ALGEBRA & MATH

Python Solutions for 100 Algebra and 100 Physics Questions

- Improve your coding skills
- Code your algebra and physics skills
- Python programming for advanced

D1568844

Published by Creatspace: 15/08/2020

ISBN-13 : 979-8666011294

Farukh Khalilov
Bilal Sengez
Fatih Narin
Tayyip Oral

ALGEBRA & MATH

Python Solutions for 100 Algebra and 100 Physics Questions

- Improve your coding skills
- Code your algebra and physics skills
- Python programming for advanced

Book design and interior formatting by Sahib Kazimov
e-mail: kazimli@hotmail.com

555 Math Book series

1) 1000 Logic & Reasoning Questions for Gifted and Talented Elementary School Students

2) 555 SAT Math(555 Questions with Solution)

3) 555 GEOMETRY (555 Questions with Solution)

4) 555 GEOMETRY Problems for High School Students

5) 555 ACT Math (555 Questions with Solution)

6) 555 ACT Math (555 Questions with Answers)

7) 555 ADVANCED Math Problems - for Middle School Students

8) 555 MATH IQ Questions for High School Students

9) 555 MATH IQ Questions for Middle School Students

10) 555 MATH IQ Questions for Elementary School Students

11) 555 GEOMETRY Formula handbook for SAT, ACT, GRE

12) GEOMETRY Formula Handbook

13) ALGEBRA Handbook for Middle School Students

14) GEOMETRY for SAT&ACT (555 Questions with Answers)

15) 555 Gifted and Talented for Middle School Students

16) ALGEBRA for the New SAT (1111 Questions with Answers)

17) TSI MATH (Texas Success Initiative)

18) CLEP College Algebra

19) Math Coding (Python Solutions for 150 Math Questions)

Preface

This book is designed for High school students and advanced programming language learners. Computer science has continuously escalated in popularity over the last decade, as students are increasingly showing interest in coding at a young age. In this book you will find a total of 200 Algebra and Physics questions, ranging in difficulty from beginner to advanced, with accompanying Python programming language solutions. Python is one of the most popular coding languages and is comparatively easy to learn. With this book, students will be able to increase their proficiency in coding and math computing. This book can be used as a reference for math and computer science teachers for interdisciplinary purposes and will help students improve their skills and critical thinking. Two hundred of question and solution implementation case studies give students engaging python program. This book help you supports Algebra and Physics, career opportunities. You will learn by this book in artificial intelligence, wed development , and machine learning.

Farukh Khalilov, Bilal Sengez, Fatih Narin, Tayyip Oral

Contact e-mail: oral_tayyip@yahoo.com

ALGEBRA

Python Solutions
for
100 Algebra Questions

Note: *All images in Algebra section (s) are not in high quality since they are all generated from the codes given in this book.*

1. **If *2x+5=11* then *x=?***

```
import sympy as sym
from IPython.display import display, Math

x = sym.symbols('x')

exp = 2*x + 5 - 11

solution = sym.solve(exp)

display(Math('\\text{The solution for } %s \\text{ = 0 is } %s'
            %(sym.latex(exp), sym.latex(solution[0])))))
```

The solution for 2x−6 = 0 is 3

2. **If *2n–23=98* then *n=?***

```
import sympy as sym
from IPython.display import display, Math

n = sym.symbols('n')

exp = 2*n - 23 - 98

solution = sym.solve(exp)

display(Math('\\text{The solution for } %s \\text{ = 0 is } %s'
            %(sym.latex(exp), sym.latex(solution[0])))))
```

The solution for 2n−121 = 0 is $\frac{121}{2}$

3. **If $a^2-4=0$ then $a=?$**

```
import sympy as sym
from IPython.display import display, Math

a = sym.symbols('a')

exp = a**2 - 4

solution = sym.solve(exp)

for i in range(0,len(solution)):
    display(Math('\\text{The solution number }'
                '%s\\text{ for } %s \\text{ = 0 is } %s'
                %(str(i+1), sym.latex(exp),solution[i])))
```

The solution number 1 for $a^2-4 = 0$ is -2
The solution number 2 for $a^2-4 = 0$ is 2

4. **Simplify and solve the following equation** *(Display your solution).*

$$3b+\frac{2}{b}+5=5b+\frac{1}{b}-1$$

```
import sympy as sym
from IPython.display import display, Math

b = sym.symbols('b')

exp = 3*b + 2/b + 5 - 5*b - 1/b + 1
solution = sym.solve(exp)

display(Math('\\text{The simplest form is } %s'
            %sym.latex(exp)))
display(Math('\\text{The solutions are } %s'
            %sym.latex(sym.solve(exp))))
```

The simplest form is $-2b+6+\dfrac{1}{b}$

The solutions are $\left[\dfrac{3}{2}-\dfrac{\sqrt{11}}{2},\ \dfrac{3}{2}+\dfrac{\sqrt{11}}{2}\right]$

5. **Simplify and solve the following equation** *(Display your solution).*

$2x+3y–25=0$ **where** $y=x+1$

```
import sympy as sym
from IPython.display import display, Math

x,y = sym.symbols('x,y')

exp = 2*x + 3*y - 25
suby = x + 1

new_exp = exp.subs(y,suby)

display(Math('\\text{ if %s = 0 and y = %s}'%(sym.latex(exp),
            sym.latex(suby))))
display(Math('\\text{Then x = } %s' %sym.latex(sym.solve(new_exp))))
```

if 2x+3y–25=0 and y=x+1 Then $x = \left[\dfrac{22}{5} \right]$

6. **Simplify the following expression:**

$$2p+3p^2 - \frac{5}{p} - \frac{4}{p^3}$$

```
import sympy as sym
from IPython.display import display, Math

p = sym.symbols('p')

exp = 2*p + 3*p**2 - 5/p - 4/(p**3)

display(Math(sym.latex(sym.cancel(exp))))
```

$$\frac{3p^5 + 2p^4 - 5p^2 - 4}{p^3}$$

7. **Simplify the following equation**:

$$\frac{\sqrt{3} + \sqrt{15b}}{\sqrt{2} + \sqrt{10b}}$$

```python
import sympy as sym
from IPython.display import display, Math

b = sym.symbols('b')
exp = (sym.sqrt(3) + sym.sqrt(15) * b) / (sym.sqrt(2) +
sym.sqrt(10)*b)

display(Math('\\text{The simple form of }%s \\Rightarrow %s'
            %(sym.latex(exp), sym.latex(sym.simplify(exp)))))
```

The simple form of $\dfrac{\sqrt{15}b + \sqrt{3}}{\sqrt{10}b + \sqrt{2}} \Rightarrow \dfrac{\sqrt{6}}{2}$

8. **Simplify the following rational expression**:

$$\frac{4a^2 + 4ab + b^2}{8a + 4b}$$

```python
import sympy as sym
from IPython.display import display, Math

a,b = sym.symbols('a,b')
exp = (4*a**2 + 4*b*a + b**2) / (8*a + 4*b)
display(Math('\\text{The simple form of }%s \\Rightarrow %s'
            %(sym.latex(exp), sym.latex(sym.simplify(exp)))))
```

The simple form of $\dfrac{4a^2 + 4ab + b^2}{8a + 4b} \Rightarrow \dfrac{a}{2} + \dfrac{b}{4}$

9. **Simplify the following rational expression:**

$$\frac{3t^6 + 21t^4}{t^4 + 11t^2 + 28}$$

```python
import sympy as sym
from IPython.display import display, Math

t = sym.symbols('t')
exp = (3*t**6 + 21*t**4) / (t**4 + 11*t**2 + 28)
display(Math('\\text{The simple form of }%s \\Rightarrow %s'
            %(sym.latex(exp), sym.latex(sym.simplify(exp)))))
```

The simple form of $\dfrac{3t^6 + 21t^4}{t^4 + 11t + 28} \Rightarrow \dfrac{3t^4}{t^2 + 4}$

10. **Expand the following expression:**

$$a\left(\frac{-5^a}{a} + 2b^2\right)$$

```python
import sympy as sym
from IPython.display import display,Math

a,b = sym.symbols('a,b')

exp = a * ((-5**a)/a + 2*(b**2))

display(Math('%s \\Rightarrow%s'
            %(sym.latex(exp),sym.latex(sym.expand(exp)))))
```

$a\left(-\dfrac{5^a}{a} + 2b^2\right) \Rightarrow -5^a + 2ab^2$

11. Expand the following expression:

$$(x+y)^3$$

```python
import sympy as sym
from IPython.display import display,Math

x,y = sym.symbols('x,y')

exp = (x + y)**3

display(Math('%s \\Rightarrow %s'
        %(sym.latex(exp),sym.latex(sym.expand(exp)))))
```

$$(x+y)^3 \Rightarrow x^3 + 3x^2y + 3xy^2 + y^3$$

12. Expand the following expression:

$$(2a+b)(a^2-3b)$$

```python
import sympy as sym
from IPython.display import display,Math

a,b = sym.symbols('a,b')

exp1 = 2*a + b
exp2 = a**2 - 3*b

display(Math('(%s)(%s) \\Rightarrow  %s'
        %(sym.latex(exp1),sym.latex(exp2),
        sym.latex(sym.expand(exp1*exp2)))))
```

$$(2a+b)(a^2-3b) \Rightarrow 2a^3 + a^2b - 6ab - 3b^2$$

13. Multiply two expressions: $2a^2+3ab+b^2$ and $a+5$

```
import sympy as sym
from IPython.display import display, Math

a,b = sym.symbols('a,b')

exp1 = 2*a**2 + 3*a*b + b**2
exp2 = a + 5

display(Math('(%s)\\times(%s) \\Rightarrow %s'
            %(sym.latex(exp1),sym.latex(exp2),
            sym.latex(sym.expand(exp1*exp2))) ))
```

$(2a^2+3ab+b^2)\times(a+5) \Rightarrow 2a^3+3a^2b+10a^2+ab^2+15ab+5b^2$

14. $f(x)=x^2+5$ if $x=10$, then $f(x)=?$

```
import sympy as sym
from IPython.display import display, Math

x = sym.symbols('x')

exp = x**2 + 5

display(Math('\\text{For expression }%s,'
            '\\text{when x = 10, then f(10) = }%s'
            %(sym.latex(exp),sym.latex(exp.subs({x:10})))))
```

For expression x^2+5, when x=10, then f(10)=105

15. $f(x)=2x^3-4x$. **Solve** $f(x)$ **for all values of** $x=(-2, -1, 0, 1, 2)$

```python
import sympy as sym
from IPython.display import display, Math

x = sym.symbols('x')
exp = 2*x**3 -4*x
for i in range(-2,3):
    display(Math('\\text{When x = }%s \\Rightarrow'
                 '\\text{f(x) = }%s '
                 %(i, sym.latex(exp.subs({x:i})))))
```

When x=−2 ⇒ f(x)=−8
When x=−1 ⇒ f(x)=2
When x=0 ⇒ f(x)=0
When x=1 ⇒ f(x)=−2
When x=2 ⇒ f(x)=8

16. Which value of $x=(1, 2, 3, 4)$ **should be replaced in following expresion that** $f(x)$ **will be equal to zero?**

```python
import sympy as sym
from IPython.display import display, Math

x = sym.symbols('x')
exp = -2*x**2 + 8
for i in range(0,5):
    if exp.subs(x,i) == 0:
        display(Math('\\text{If x = }%s \\Rightarrow'
                     '\\text{f(x) = }%s'
                     %(i, sym.latex(exp.subs({x:i})))))
```

If x=2 ⇒ f(x) = 0

17. If $g(x)=x^3-7x^2+22$ from the set A, what value of x should be that the result of $g(x)$ is positive? *set A = (-20, -19, ... 19, 20)*

```
import sympy as sym

x = sym.symbols('x')

exp = x**3 - 7*x**2 + 22
new_set = []
for i in range(-12,13):
    if exp.subs(x,i) > 0:
        new_set.append(i)
print("From the given set A, only following values"
      "of x gives g(x) the positive result: %s"
      %new_set)
```

From the given set A, only following values of x gives g(x) the positive result: [-1, 0, 1, 2, 7, 8, 9, 10, 11, 12]

18. $f(x, y)=(3+x)(4-y)$. **Solve** $f(x, y)$ **for all values of** $x, y=(0, 1, 2)$

Display all solutions.

```
import sympy as sym
from IPython.display import display, Math

x,y = sym.symbols('x,y')

exp = (3+x)*(4-y)

for i in range(0,3):
    for j in range(0,3):
        display(Math('\\text{When x = }%s \\text{ and y = }%s,'
                     '\\Rightarrow \\text{ f(x,y) =}%s'
                     %(i,j,sym.latex(exp.subs({x:i,y:j})))))
```

When x = 0 and y = 0, $\Rightarrow$ f(x,y) =12   When x = 0 and y = 1, $\Rightarrow$ f(x,y) =9
When x = 0 and y = 2, $\Rightarrow$ f(x,y) =6   When x = 1 and y = 0, $\Rightarrow$ f(x,y) =16
When x = 1 and y = 1, $\Rightarrow$ f(x,y) =12   When x = 1 and y = 2, $\Rightarrow$ f(x,y) =8
When x = 2 and y = 0, $\Rightarrow$ f(x,y) =20   When x = 2 and y = 1, $\Rightarrow$ f(x,y) =15
When x = 2 and y = 2, $\Rightarrow$ f(x,y) =10

19. Multiply and expand following equations:

$$f_1 = x(y+z) \text{ and } f_2 = \frac{3}{x} + x^2 \text{ where } x = a(3+a) + \frac{2}{a^2}(2-a)$$

```
import sympy as sym
from IPython.display import display, Math

x,y,z,a = sym.symbols('x,y,z,a')

f1 = x*(y+z)
f2 = 3/x + x**2
replace_x = a*(3+a) + (2/(a**2))*(2-a)

display(Math('$f_1 \\times f_2 = %s$' %sym.latex((f1*f2))))
display(Math(sym.latex((f1*f2).subs({x:replace_x}))))
display(Math(sym.latex(sym.simplify((f1*f2).subs({x:replace_x})))))
```

$$f_1 \times f_2 = x\left(x^2 + \frac{3}{x}\right)(y+z)$$

$$(y+z)\left(a(a+3) + \frac{2(2-a)}{a^2}\right)\left(\left(a(a+3) + \frac{2(2-a)}{a^2}\right)^2 + \frac{3}{a(a+3) + \frac{2(2-a)}{a^2}}\right)$$

$$\frac{\left(3a^6 + (a^3(a+3) - 2a + 4)^3\right)(y+z)}{a^6}$$

20. Find the Greatest Common Denominator of following numbers: 45 and 15.

```
import math
math.gcd(45,15)
```

15

21. Find the Greatest Common Denominator of following numbers: -9 and 18.

```python
import math
math.gcd(-9,18)
```

9

22. Find the Greatest Common Denominator of following set of numbers:

set A = [(15,12)(18,12)(24,16)(27,63)]

```python
import math

set_A = [(15,12),(18,12),(24,16),(27,63)]

for i in range(0, len(set_A)):
    print(math.gcd(set_A[i][0],set_A[i][1]))
```

3
6
8
9

23. Simplify the following fraction and display all steps:

$$\frac{8}{48}$$

```python
import math
from IPython.display import display, Math

a = 8
b = 48
fact = math.gcd(8,48)

display(Math('\\frac{%g}{%g} = \\frac{%g \\times %g}{%g'
            '\\times %g} = \\frac{%g}{%g}'
            %(a,b,a/fact,fact,b/fact,fact,a/fact,b/fact)))
```

$$\frac{8}{48} = \frac{1 \times 8}{6 \times 8} = \frac{1}{6}$$

24. Simplify the following fraction and display all steps:

$$\frac{245}{155}$$

```python
import math
from IPython.display import display, Math

a = 245
b = 155
fact = math.gcd(245,155)

display(Math('\\frac{%g}{%g} = \\frac{%g \\times %g}{%g'
            '\\times %g} = \\frac{%g}{%g}'
            %(a,b,a/fact,fact,b/fact,fact,a/fact,b/fact)))
```

$$\frac{245}{155} = \frac{49 \times 5}{31 \times 5} = \frac{49}{31}$$

25. Illustrate the following property using symbolic variables and show an example with numbers.

$gcd(zx,zy)=zgcd(x,y)$ (gcd = **Greatest common denominator**)

```python
import math
import sympy as sym

x,y,z = sym.symbols('x,y,z')

print(sym.gcd(x*z, y*z))
print(z*sym.gcd(x,y))

# using numbers
x = 12
y = 4
z = 6
print(math.gcd(x*z, y*z))
print(z*math.gcd(x,y))
```

z
z
24
24

26. **Find out if 48 is a prime number.**

```python
import sympy as sym
number = 48

di = sym.factorint(number)
ks = list(di.keys())

if len(di) == 1 and di[ks[0]] == 1:
    print("This is a prime number")
else:
    print("Is not a prime number")
```

Is not a prime number

27. Print only prime numbers from the given list A

A = (-5, -4, ... 4, 5)

```
new_list = []
for i in range(-5,6):
    di = sym.factorint(i)
    ks = list(di.keys())

    if len(di) == 1 and di[ks[0]] == 1:
        new_list.append(i)
print(new_list)
```

[-1, 0, 2, 3, 5]

28. From the given set A, determine each value "Prime" or "Composite"

Set A = (5,6,...14,15)

```
for i in range(5,16):
    di = sym.factorint(i)
    ks = list(di.keys())

    if len(di) == 1 and di[ks[0]] == 1:
        print('%s is a prime number'%i)
    else:
        print('%s is a composite number'%i)
```

5 is a prime number   6 is a composite number
7 is a prime number   8 is a composite number
9 is a composite number   10 is a composite number
11 is a prime number   12 is a composite number
13 is a prime number   14 is a composite number
15 is a composite number

29. Print prime numbers from the given list A:

A = (34, 26, 74, 12, 11, 35, 96, 23, 27)

```python
import sympy as sym

list_A = [34,26,74,12,11,35,96,23,27]
new_list = []
for i in list_A:
    di = sym.factorint(i)
    ks = list(di.keys())

    if len(di) == 1 and di[ks[0]] == 1:
        new_list.append(i)
print(new_list)
```

[11, 23]

30. How many prime numbers are between 1 and 100?

```python
import sympy as sym

sum = 0
for i in range(1,101):
    di = sym.factorint(i)
    ks = list(di.keys())

    if len(di) == 1 and di[ks[0]] == 1:
        sum = sum + 1
print(sum)
```

25

31. How many prime and composite number between 1 and 250?

```python
import sympy as sym

prime_sum = 0
composite_sum = 0
for i in range(1,251):
    di = sym.factorint(i)
    ks = list(di.keys())

    if len(di) == 1 and di[ks[0]] == 1:
        prime_sum = prime_sum + 1
    else:
        composite_sum = composite_sum + 1

print("There are %s primer numbers and %s composite numbers"
      %(prime_sum,composite_sum))
```

There are 53 primer numbers and 197 composite numbers

32. Solve the following inequality: *3x>12*

```python
import sympy as sym

x = sym.symbols('x')

exp = 3*x > 12

print(sym.solve(exp))
```

$(4 < x)\ \&\ (x < \infty)$

33. Solve the following inequality: $40 \leq a+3$

```python
import sympy as sym

a = sym.symbols('a')

exp = 40 <= a + 3

print(sym.solve(exp))
```

$(37 \leq a)$ & $(a < \infty)$

34. Solve the following equation: $-2(x^2-12)-142=0$

```python
import sympy as sym
from IPython.display import display,Math

x = sym.symbols('x')

exp = -2*(x**2 -12) - 142

display(Math(sym.latex(sym.solve(exp))))
```

$\left[-\sqrt{59}i, \sqrt{59}i\right]$

35. Solve the following inequality: $(a-1)(a+4)>0$

```
import sympy as sym
from IPython.display import display, Math

a = sym.symbols('a')

exp = (a-1)*(a+4) > 0

display(Math(sym.latex(sym.solve(exp))))
```

$(-\infty < a \wedge a < -4) \vee (1 < a \wedge a < \infty)$

36. Simplify and solve the following inequality:

$$\frac{2x}{3} + \frac{3-7x}{4} \leq 2 - \frac{4(3-x)}{4}$$

```
import sympy as sym
from IPython.display import display, Math
x = sym.symbols('x')
exp = ((2*x)/3 + (3-7*x)/4) <= 2 - (4*(3-x)/4)
display(Math('\\text{The simple form is }%s'%sym.latex(exp)))
display(Math('\\text{The solution is }%s'
            %sym.latex(sym.solve(exp))))
```

The simple form is $\dfrac{3}{4} - \dfrac{13x}{12} \leq x-1$

The solution is $\dfrac{21}{25} \leq x \wedge x < \infty$

37. Add the following two polynomials and print result:

Polynomial 1: $x^3 + 2x - 4$
Polynomial 2: $-x^2 + x + 1$

```python
import sympy as sym
from IPython.display import display, Math


x = sym.symbols('x')


p1 = x**3 + 2*x - 4
p2 = -x**2 + x + 1


display(Math('(%s) + (%s) = %s'
            %(sym.latex(p1),sym.latex(p2),sym.latex(p1+p2))))
```

$(x^3+2x-4)+(-x^2+x+1)=x^3-x^2+3x-3$

38. Subtract the following two polynomials and print result:

Polynomial 1: $a^2 + 3a - 5$
Polynomial 2: $2a^2 - 3a + 5$

```python
import sympy as sym
from IPython.display import display, Math


a = sym.symbols('a')


p1 = a**2 + 3*a - 5
p2 = 2*a**2 - 3*a + 5


display(Math('(%s) - (%s) = %s'
            %(sym.latex(p1),sym.latex(p2),sym.latex(p1-p2))))
```

$(a^2 + 3a - 5) - (2a^2 - 3a + 5) = -a^2 + 6a - 10$

39. Multiply the polynomials. (Display all steps)

$$f(a,b)=4a^4-3a^2+ab^2-9b^3$$
$$g(a,b)=-a^3+6a^2b+b^3$$

```
import sympy as sym
from IPython.display import display, Math

a,b = sym.symbols('a,b')

f = 4*a**4 - 3*a**2 + a*b**2 - 9*b**3
g = -a**3 + 6*a**2*b + b**3

display(Math('\\text{f(a,b)} = %s'%sym.latex(f)))
display(Math('\\text{g(a,b)} = %s'%sym.latex(g)))
display(Math('\\text{f(a,b)} \\times \\text{g(a,b) = }%s'
        %sym.latex(f*g)))
display(Math('\\text{f(a,b)} \\times \\text{g(a,b) = }%s'
        %sym.latex(sym.expand(f*g))))
```

$f(a,b)= 4a^4-3a^2+ab^2-9b^3$

$g(a,b)= -a^3+6a^2b+b^3$

$f(a,b){\times}g(a,b)=(-a^3+6a^2b+b^3){\times}(4a^4-3a^2+ab^2-9b^3)$

$f(a,b){\times}g(a,b)=-4a^7+24a^6b+3a^5+4a^4b^3-a^4b^2-18a^4b+15a^3b^3-54a^2b^4-3a^2b^3+ab^5-9b^6$

40. Expand the following polynomial (Display All steps).

$$y=(a+b)^4$$

```
import sympy as sym
from IPython.display import display, Math

a,b = sym.symbols('a,b')

y = (a+b)**4

display(Math('%s \\Rightarrow %s' %(sym.latex(y),
        sym.latex(sym.expand(y)))))
```

$(a+b)^4 \Rightarrow a^4 + 4a^3b + 6a^2b^2 + 4ab^3 + b^4$

41. Multiply the polynomials and THEN substitute x= 5 and y = -4. (Display all steps).

$f(x,y)=3x^3-7x^2-xy+5y^2$
$g(x,y)=5x^2+4xy-y^3$

```python
import sympy as sym
from IPython.display import display, Math

x,y = sym.symbols('x,y')

f = 3*x**3 - 7*x**2 - x*y + 5*y**2
g = 5*x**2 + 4*x*y - y**3

display(Math('\\text{f(a,b)} = %s'%sym.latex(f)))
display(Math('\\text{g(a,b)} = %s'%sym.latex(g)))
display(Math('\\text{f(a,b)} \\times \\text{g(a,b) = }%s'
            %sym.latex(f*g)))
display(Math('\\text{f(a,b)} \\times \\text{g(a,b) = }%s'
            %sym.latex(sym.expand(f*g))))

# Substitute x = 5 and y = -4
result = f*g
display(Math('\\text{if x = 5 and y = -4 then f(a,b)}'
            '\\times \\text{g(a,b) = }%s'
            %sym.latex(result.subs({x:5,y:-4}))))
```

$f(a,b)=3x^3-7x^2-xy+5y^2$

$g(a,b)=5x^2+4xy-y^3$

$f(a,b)\times g(a,b) = (5x^2+4xy-y^3)(3x^3-7x^2-xy+5y^2)$

$f(a,b)\times g(a,b) = 15x^5+12x^4y-35x^4-3x^3y^3-33x^3y+7x^2y^3+21x^2y^2+xy^4+20xy^3-5y^5$

if x=5 and y=−4 then f(a,b)×g(a,b) = 32700

42. Substitute the polynomials and THEN multiply m = -2 and n = 7 (Display all steps).

$h(m, n) = -2m^5 + 4m^4 - 2mn + 8n^2$

$g(m, n) = -3m^2 - 4mn + 3n^2$

```python
import sympy as sym
from IPython.display import display, Math

m,n = sym.symbols('m,n')

h = -2*m**5 + 4*m**4 - 2*m*n + 8*n**2
g = -3*m**2 - 4*m*n + 3*n**2

# substitute m=-2 and n=7

hsub = h.subs({m:-2, n:7})
gsub = g.subs({m:-2, n:7})

display(Math('h(m,n) = %s'%sym.latex(h)))
display(Math('g(m,n) = %s'%sym.latex(g)))
display(Math('h(-2,7) = %s'%hsub))
display(Math('g(-2,7) = %s'%gsub))

display(Math('h(-2,7) \\times g(-2,7) = %s'%(hsub*gsub)))
```

$h(m, n) = -2m^5 + 4m^4 - 2mn + 8n^2$

$g(m, n) = -3m^2 - 4mn + 3n^2$

$h(-2, 7) = 548$

$g(-2, 7) = 191$

$h(-2, 7) \times g(-2, 7) = 104668$

43. Divide and simplify two polynomials (Display All steps).

$y_1 = 4a^5 - a$
$y_1 = 2a^3 - a$

```
import sympy as sym
from IPython.display import display, Math

a = sym.symbols('a')
y1 = 4*a**5 - a
y2 = 2*a**3 - a

display(Math('\\frac{%s}{%s} = %s'%(sym.latex(y1),sym.latex(y2),
            sym.latex(sym.expand(y1/y2)))))
display(Math('\\frac{%s}{%s} = %s'%(sym.latex(y1),sym.latex(y2),
            sym.latex(sym.simplify(y1/y2)))))
```

$$\frac{4a^5 - a}{2a^3 - a} = \frac{4a^5}{2a^3 - a} - \frac{a}{2a^3 - a}$$

$$\frac{4a^5 - a}{2a^3 - a} = 2a^2 + 1$$

44. Expand the following polynomial: $y = (2x+3)^2$

```
import sympy as sym
from IPython.display import display, Math

x = sym.symbols('x')

y = (2*x + 3)**2

display(Math('%s \\Rightarrow %s' %(sym.latex(y),
            sym.latex(sym.expand(y)))))
```

$(2x+3)^2 \Rightarrow 4x^2 + 12x + 9$

45. **For the following polynomial division, which the value of b must be that elminates the denominator (at the result it should NOT be fractional polynomial)**

$$\frac{a^6 + 2a^4 + 6a - b}{a^3 + 3} \quad \text{where } b = (5, 6, \dots, 14, 15)$$

```python
import sympy as sym
from IPython.display import display, Math

a,b = sym.symbols('a,b')

Numerator = a**6 + 2*a**4 + 6*a - b
Denominator = a**3 + 3

for bi in range(5,11):
    tempnum = Numerator.subs(b,bi)
    display(Math('%s = %s' %(sym.latex(tempnum/Denominator),
                 sym.latex(sym.simplify(tempnum/Denominator)))))
    if sym.fraction(sym.simplify(tempnum/Denominator))[1] == 1:
        rightanswer = bi

print("The value of b should be equal to %g that eliminates
    the denominator." %rightanswer)
```

$$\frac{a^6 + 2a^4 + 6a - 5}{a^3 + 3} = \frac{a^6 + 2a^4 + 6a - 5}{a^3 + 3}$$

$$\frac{a^6 + 2a^4 + 6a - 6}{a^3 + 3} = \frac{a^6 + 2a^4 + 6a - 6}{a^3 + 3}$$

$$\frac{a^6 + 2a^4 + 6a - 7}{a^3 + 3} = \frac{a^6 + 2a^4 + 6a - 7}{a^3 + 3}$$

$$\frac{a^6 + 2a^4 + 6a - 8}{a^3 + 3} = \frac{a^6 + 2a^4 + 6a - 8}{a^3 + 3}$$

$$\frac{a^6 + 2a^4 + 6a - 9}{a^3 + 3} = a^3 + 2a - 3$$

$$\frac{a^6 + 2a^4 + 6a - 10}{a^3 + 3} = \frac{a^6 + 2a^4 + 6a - 10}{a^3 + 3}$$

The value of b should be equal to 9 that eliminates the denominator.

46. Factorize the following expression: $a^3 + 9a^2$

```python
import sympy as sym
from IPython.display import display,Math

a,b = sym.symbols('a,b')
exp = a**3 + 9*a**2

display(Math(sym.latex(exp)))
display(Math(sym.latex(sym.factor(exp))))
```

$a^3 + 9a^2$

$a^2(a + 9)$

47. Factorize the following expression: $125m^3 - 27n^3$

```python
import sympy as sym
from IPython.display import display,Math

m,n = sym.symbols('m,n')
exp = 125*m**3 - 27*n**3

display(Math(sym.latex(exp)))
display(Math(sym.latex(sym.factor(exp))))
```

$125m^3 - 27n^3$

$(5m - 3n)(25m^2 + 15mn + 9n^2)$

48. Factorize the following expression:

$2a^3b - 2a^2 + 2a^2b + 6a^2 - 6ab + 6a$

```python
import sympy as sym
from IPython.display import display,Math

a,b = sym.symbols('a,b')
exp = 2*a**3*b - 2*a**2 + 2*a**2*b + 6*a**2 - 6*a*b + 6*a

display(Math(sym.latex(exp)))
display(Math(sym.latex(sym.factor(exp))))
```

$2a^3b + 2a^2b + 4a^2 - 6ab + 6a$

$2a(a^2b + ab + 2a - 3b + 3)$

49. Determine wheter the following polynomials can be factored:

$a^2 + 4a + 3$
$2b^2 - 1$
$3b^2 + 12b$

```python
import sympy as sym
from IPython.display import display,Math

a,b = sym.symbols('a,b')

exp = [a**2 + 4*a + 3 , 2*b - 1 , 3*b**2 + 12*b]

for i in exp:
    if str(sym.factor(i)).find('(') != -1:
        display(Math('%s \\Rightarrow %s '
                    %(sym.latex(i),
                        sym.latex(sym.factor(i)))))
    else:
        display(Math('%s \\Rightarrow \\text{ Not factorable}'
                %sym.latex(i)))
```

$a^2 + 4a + 3 \Rightarrow (a+1)(a+3)$
$2b - 1 \Rightarrow$ Not factorable
$3b^2 + 12b \Rightarrow 3b(b+4)$

50. Replace each value of y = (8,9,...12,13) in following expression and find out the which value can help factorize the expression.

$2x^2 - 5x - y$

```
import sympy as sym
from IPython.display import display,Math

x,y = sym.symbols('x,y')

exp = 2*x**2 - 5*x - y
display(Math(sym.latex(exp)))
for i in range(8,14):
    display(Math('\\text{If y = }%s \\Rightarrow %s'
                 %(i, sym.latex(sym.factor(exp.subs({y:i}))))))
```

$2x^2 - 5x - y$

If $y = 8 \Rightarrow 2x^2 - 5x - 8$

If $y = 9 \Rightarrow 2x^2 - 5x - 9$

If $y = 10 \Rightarrow 2x^2 - 5x - 10$

If $y = 11 \Rightarrow 2x^2 - 5x - 11$

If $y = 12 \Rightarrow (x-4)(2x+3)$

If $y = 13 \Rightarrow 2x^2 - 5x - 13$

51. Plot all points for $y=x^2-4x$ **where** $x = \{-10, -9, -8, \ldots 10, 11\}$.

```python
import matplotlib.pyplot as plt

setx = []
sety = []

for i in range(-10,12):
    setx.append(i)
    y = i**2 - 4*i
    sety.append(y)

for i in range(0,len(setx)):
    plt.plot(setx[i],sety[i],'o')

plt.grid()
plt.show()
```

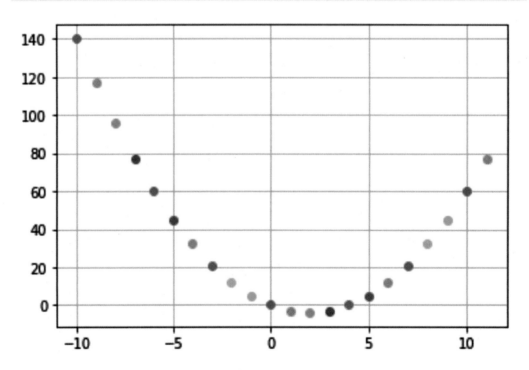

52. Plot all points for $y = \dfrac{3x^3}{2} + 1$ **where** $x = \{-10, -9, -8, \dots 19, 20\}$

```python
import matplotlib.pyplot as plt

setx = []
sety = []

for n in range(-10,21):
    setx.append(n)
    y = 3*n**3/2 + 1
    sety.append(y)

for n in range(0,len(setx)):
    plt.plot(setx[n],sety[n],'+')

plt.grid()
plt.show()
```

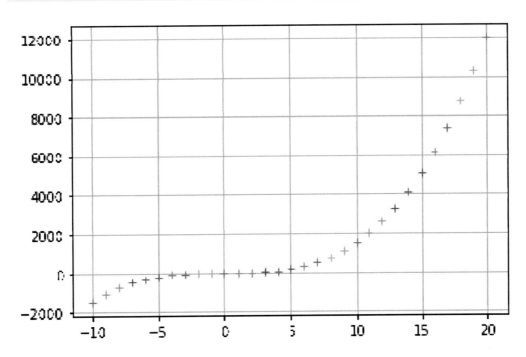

53. Plot all points for $\dfrac{\sqrt{x}}{x}$ **where** $x = \{1, 2, 3, \dots 19, 20\}$

```python
import matplotlib.pyplot as plt

setx = []
sety = []

for i in range(1,21):
    setx.append(i)
    y = (i**(1/2))/i
    sety.append(y)

for i in range(0,len(setx)):
    plt.plot(setx[i],sety[i],'s')

plt.grid()
plt.show()
```

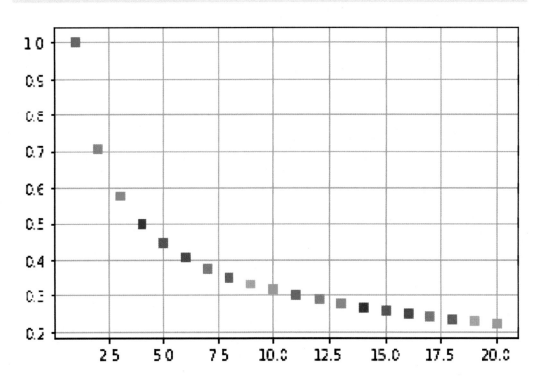

54. Plot all points for $-x^2+3x$ **where** $x = \{1, 2, 3, \dots 19, 20\}$

```python
import matplotlib.pyplot as plt

setx = []
sety = []

for i in range(1,21):
    setx.append(i)
    y = -i**2 + 3*i
    sety.append(y)

for i in range(0,len(setx)):
    plt.plot(setx[i],sety[i],'o')

plt.grid()
plt.show()
```

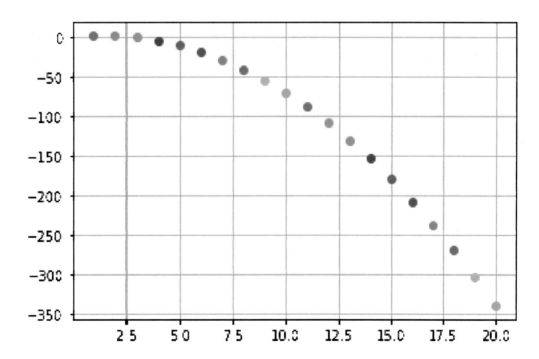

55. Plot all points for $-x^2+2x+5$ where $x = \{-20, -19, \ldots 19, 20\}$

```python
import matplotlib.pyplot as plt

setx = []
sety = []

for i in range(-20,21):
    setx.append(i)
    y = -i**2 +  2*i + 5
    sety.append(y)

for i in range(0,len(setx)):
    plt.plot(setx[i],sety[i],'x')

plt.grid()
plt.show()
```

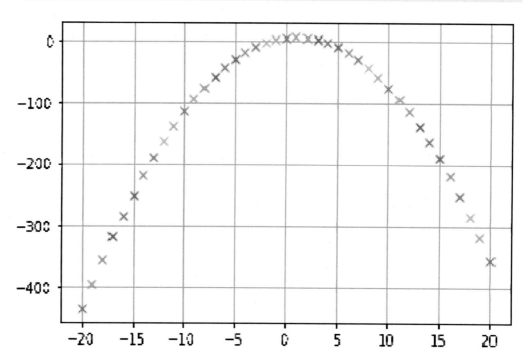

56. Display function in a math view (using sympy library) and plot all points for $y=(-4x)^2+(4x-1)$ **where** $x = \{-20, -19, \ldots 19, 20\}$

```python
import matplotlib.pyplot as plt
import sympy as sym
from IPython.display import display,Math

x,y = sym.symbols('x,y')

exp = (-4*x)**2 + (4*x - 1)

display(Math('y = %s' %sym.latex(exp)))

for i in range(-20,21):
    plt.plot(i,exp.subs({x:i}),'o')

plt.show()
```

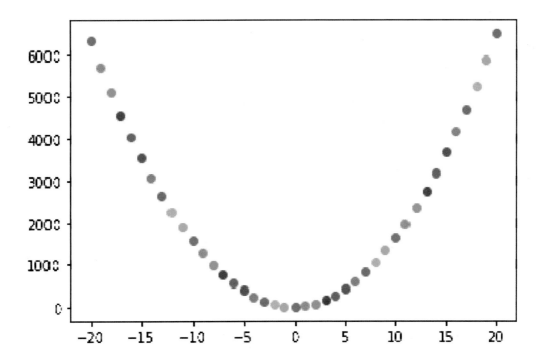

57. Display function in a math view (using sympy library) and plot all points for $y=(2x^3-9)+(x+1)$ **where** $x = \{-10, -9, ... 9, 10\}$.

```python
import matplotlib.pyplot as plt
import sympy as sym
from IPython.display import display,Math

x,y = sym.symbols('x,y')

exp = (2*x**3-9) + (x + 1)

display(Math('y = %s' %sym.latex(exp)))

for i in range(-10,11):
    plt.plot(i,exp.subs({x:i}),'o')

plt.show()
```

$y=2x^3+x-8$

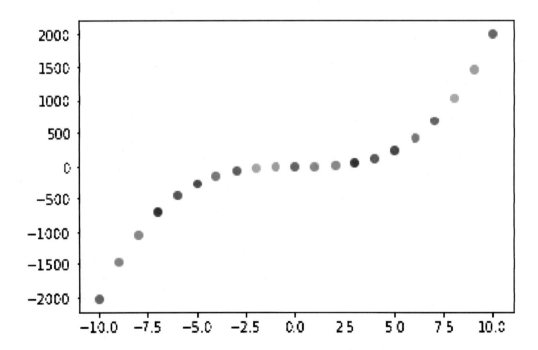

58. Display function in a math view (using sympy library) and plot all points for $y=x^4+x^3+x^2+x+1$ **where** $x = \{-10, -9, \dots 9, 10\}$.

```
import matplotlib.pyplot as plt
import sympy as sym
from IPython.display import display,Math

x,y = sym.symbols('x,y')

exp = x**4 + x**3 + x**2 + x + 1
display(Math('y = %s' %sym.latex(exp)))

for i in range(-10,11):
    plt.plot(i,exp.subs({x:i}),'*')

plt.show()
```

$y=x^4+x^3+x^2+x+1$

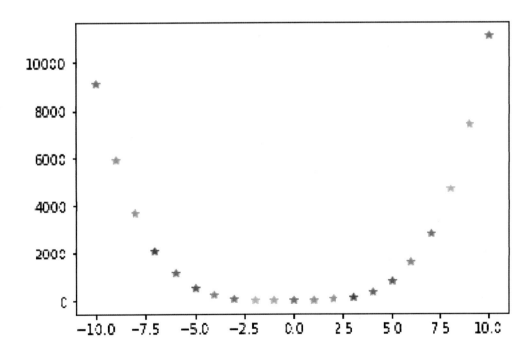

59. Display function and draw each line $y=2x^2-x$ where $x = \{-20,-19, \dots 19,20\}$

```python
import matplotlib.pyplot as plt
import sympy as sym
from IPython.display import display, Math

exp = 2*x**2-x

display(Math('y = %s' %sym.latex(exp)))

for i in range(-20,21):
    plt.plot([0,i],[0,exp.subs({x:i})])

plt.show()
```

$y=2x^2-x$

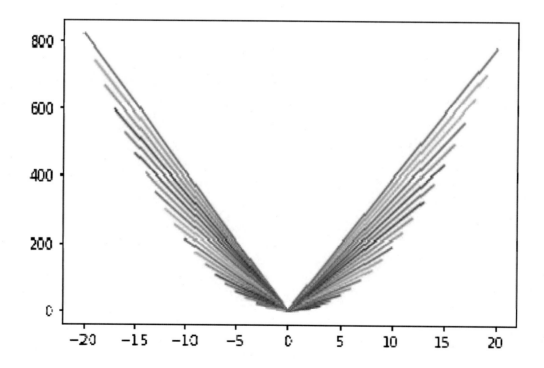

60. Display function and draw each line $y=x^3+2x$ where $x = \{-20,-19, \dots 19,20\}$

```python
import matplotlib.pyplot as plt
import sympy as sym
from IPython.display import display, Math

exp = x**3 + 2*x

display(Math('y = %s' %sym.latex(exp)))

for i in range(-20,21):
    plt.plot([0,i],[0,exp.subs({x:i})])

plt.show()
```

$y=x^3 + 2x$

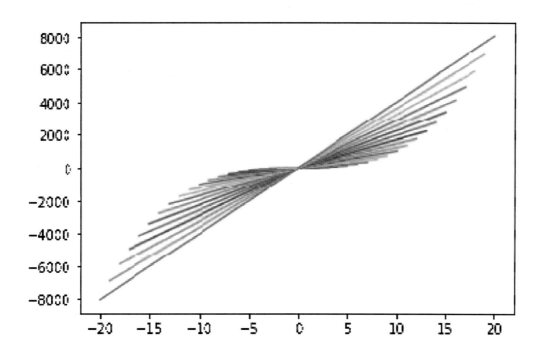

61. Display function and draw each line $y = \sqrt{x} + 1$ **where**
   $x = \{1, 2, \ldots 19, 20\}$

```python
import matplotlib.pyplot as plt
import sympy as sym
from IPython.display import display, Math

exp = x**(1/2) + 1

display(Math('y = %s' %sym.latex(exp)))

for i in range(1,21):
    plt.plot([0,i],[0,exp.subs({x:i})])

plt.show()
```

$y = x^{0.5} + 1$

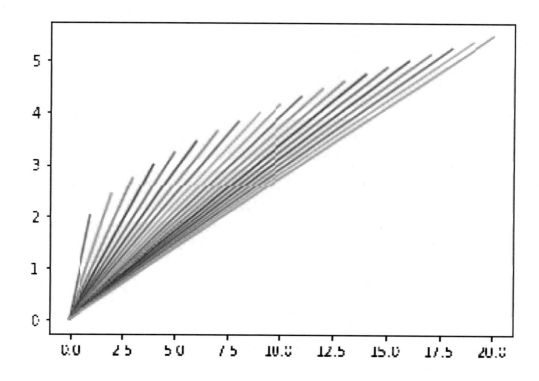

62. Display function and draw each line $y = \sqrt{|x|}$ **where**
   x = {-15,-14, ... 14,15}

```python
import matplotlib.pyplot as plt
import sympy as sym
import numpy as np
from IPython.display import display, Math

exp = abs(x)**(1/2)

display(Math('y = %s' %sym.latex(exp)))

for i in range(-15,16):
    plt.plot([0,i],[0,abs(i)**(1/2)])

plt.show()
```

$y = |x|^{0.5}$

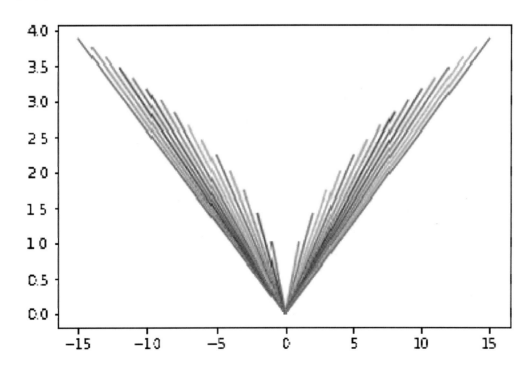

63. Display function and draw each line $y = 3 + \dfrac{1}{x}$ where

$x = \{1, 2, \dots 14, 15\}$

```python
import matplotlib.pyplot as plt
import sympy as sym
import numpy as np
from IPython.display import display, Math

exp = 3+ (1/x)

display(Math('y = %s' %sym.latex(exp)))

for i in range(1,16):
    plt.plot([0,i],[0,exp.subs({x:i})])

plt.show()
```

$$y = 3 + \frac{1}{x}$$

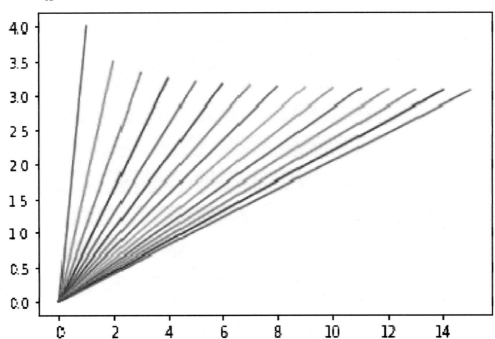

64. Display the function $y=mx+b$ **where** $m=-2$ **and** $b=-3$

```python
import matplotlib.pyplot as plt

x = [-5,5]
m = -2
b = -3

y = [1,1]

for i in range(0,len(x)):
    y[i] = m*x[i] + b

plt.plot(x,y, label = 'y = %sx+%s' %(m,b))

plt.axis('square')
plt.grid()
plt.xlim(x)
plt.ylim(x)

axis = plt.gca()

plt.plot(x,[0,0],'k--')
plt.plot([0,0],y,'k--')
plt.legend()

plt.show()
```

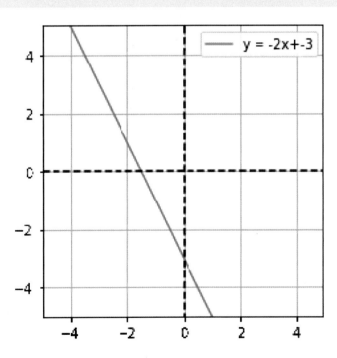

65. Display the function $y=mx+b$ **where** $m = 2$ **and** $b = 1/2$

```python
import matplotlib.pyplot as plt

x = [-5,5]
m = 2
b = 1/2

y = [1,1]

for i in range(0,len(x)):
    y[i] = m*x[i] + b

plt.plot(x,y, label = 'y = %sx+%s' %(m,b))

plt.axis('square')
plt.grid()
plt.xlim(x)
plt.ylim(x)

axis = plt.gca()

plt.plot(x,[0,0],'k--')
plt.plot([0,0],y,'k--')
plt.legend()

plt.show()
```

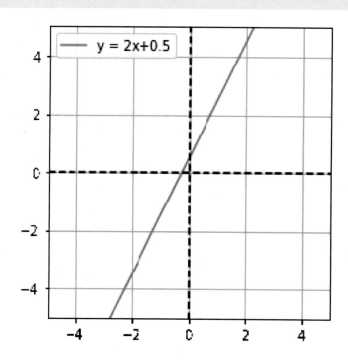

66. Display the function $y=mx+b$ **where** $m=\dfrac{1}{4}$ **and** $b=-\dfrac{2}{5}$

```python
import matplotlib.pyplot as plt

x = [-5,5]
m = 1/4
b = -2/5

y = [-4,4]

for i in range(0,len(x)):
    y[i] = m*x[i] + b

plt.plot(x,y, label = 'y = %sx+%s' %(m,b))

plt.axis('square')
plt.grid()
plt.xlim(x)
plt.ylim(x)

axis = plt.gca()

plt.plot(x,[0,0],'k--')
plt.plot([0,0],[-4,4],'k--')
plt.legend()

plt.show()
```

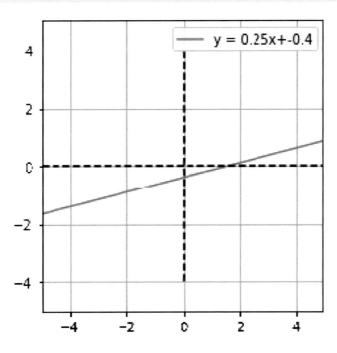

67. Display two functions *y=mx+b* where

a) m = 1 and b = -3
b) m = 2 and b = -4

```python
import matplotlib.pyplot as plt
import numpy as np

x = [-5,5]
m = [1, -3]
b = [2, -4]

for i in range(0,len(x)):
    y = m[i]*np.array(x) + b[i]
    plt.plot(x,y,label = 'y = %sx + %s' %(m[i],b[i]))

plt.axis('square')
plt.grid()
plt.xlim(x)
plt.ylim(x)

axis = plt.gca()

plt.plot(x,[0,0],'k--')
plt.plot([0,0],y,'k--')
plt.legend()

plt.show()
```

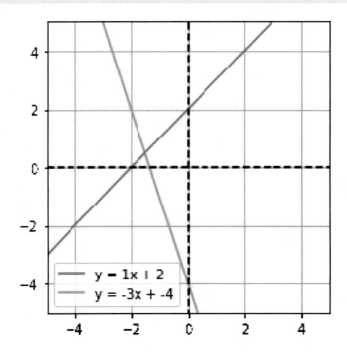

68. Graph all functions $y=-x^a$ **where** $a = (-1,0,1,2,3)$

```python
import numpy as np
import matplotlib.pyplot as plt

x = np.linspace(-4,4,200)

for i in range(-1,4):
    y = -x**i
    plt.plot(x,y,label='$y = -x^{%s}$'%i, linewidth = 4)

plt.xlim([x[0],x[-1]])
plt.ylim([-20,20])
plt.legend()

plt.show()
```

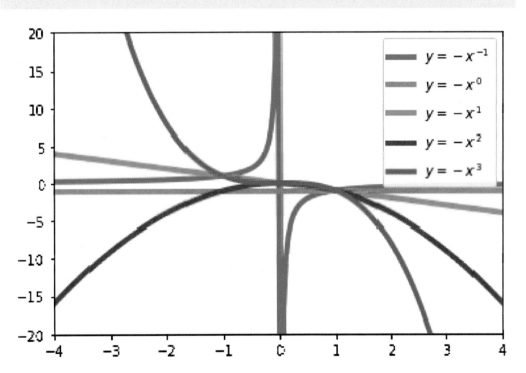

69. Graph all functions $y=ax-a$ **where** $a = (-1,0,1,2,3)$

```python
import numpy as np
import sympy as sym
import matplotlib.pyplot as plt

x = np.linspace(-4,4,200)

for i in range(-1,4):
    y = i*x - i
    plt.plot(x,y,label='$y = %s x -%s$'%(sym.latex(i),
                            sym.latex(i)), linewidth = 4)

plt.xlim([x[0],x[-1]])
plt.ylim([-20,20])
plt.legend()

plt.show()
```

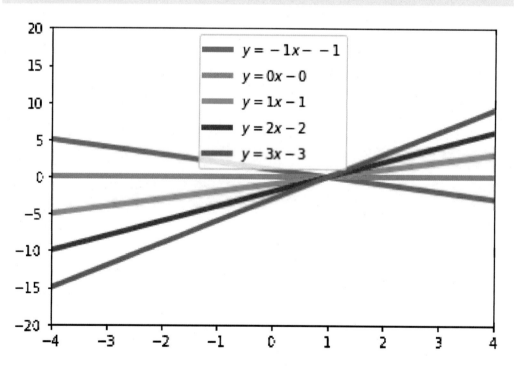

70. Graph all functions $y=x-a$ **where** $a = (-4,-3,...\ 3,4)$

```python
import numpy as np
import sympy as sym
import matplotlib.pyplot as plt

x = np.linspace(-4,4,200)

for i in range(-4,5):
    y = x - i
    plt.plot(x,y,label='$y = x -%s$'%sym.latex(i), linewidth = 4)

plt.xlim([x[0],x[-1]])
plt.ylim([-20,20])
plt.legend()

plt.show()
```

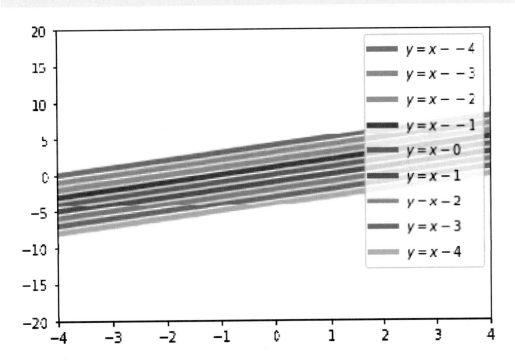

71. Displey the function $y = \dfrac{1}{2x}$ **using sympy library.**

```python
import sympy as sym
import sympy.plotting.plot as symplot

x,a = sym.symbols('x,a')

exp = 1/(2*x)
p = symplot(exp,show = False)
p.ylim = [-5,5]
p.xlim = [-5,5]
p[0].label = '$y = %s$'%sym.latex(exp)

p.legend = True
p.show()
```

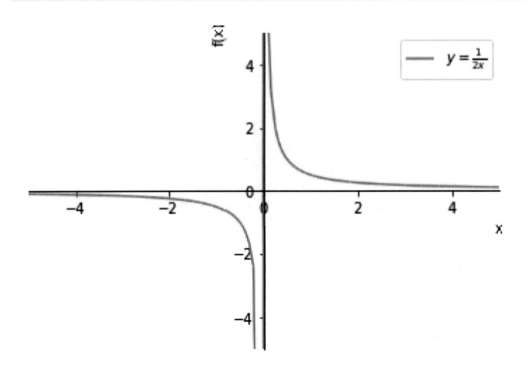

72. Displey the function $y=2x-1$ **using sympy library.**

```python
import sympy as sym
import sympy.plotting.plot as symplot

x,a = sym.symbols('x,a')

exp = x**2 - 1
p = symplot(exp,show = False)
p.ylim = [-5,5]
p.xlim = [-5,5]
p[0].label = '$y = %s$'%sym.latex(exp)

p.legend = True
p.show()
```

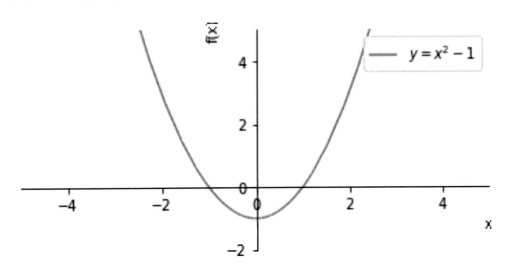

73. Displey the function $y=1-x^3$ **using sympy library.**

```python
import sympy as sym
import sympy.plotting.plot as symplot

x,a = sym.symbols('x,a')

exp = 1 - x**3
p = symplot(exp,show = False)
p.ylim = [-5,5]
p.xlim = [-5,5]
p[0].label = '$y = %s$'%sym.latex(exp)

p.legend = True
p.show()
```

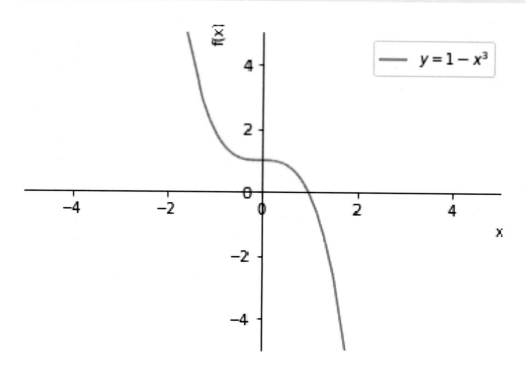

74. Displey two functions $y = \dfrac{a}{2x}$ using sympy library where $a=1$ and $a=2$.

```python
import sympy as sym
import sympy.plotting.plot as symplot

x,a = sym.symbols('x,a')

y = a/(2*x)

p = symplot(y.subs(a,1),show = False)
p.extend(symplot(y.subs(a,2),show = False))

p.ylim = [-5,5]
p.xlim = [-5,5]
p[0].label = '$y = %s$'%sym.latex(y.subs({a:1}))
p[1].label = '$y = %s$'%sym.latex(y.subs({a:2}))
p[0].line_color = 'r'

p.legend = True
p.show()
```

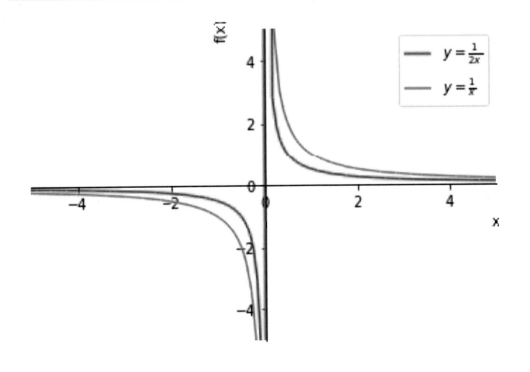

75. Displey two functions $y=x^3+a$ **using sympy library where** $a=1$ **and** $a=2$.

```python
import sympy as sym
import sympy.plotting.plot as symplot

x,a = sym.symbols('x,a')

y = x**3 + a

p = symplot(y.subs(a,1),show = False)
p.extend(symplot(y.subs(a,2),show = False))

p.ylim = [-5,5]
p.xlim = [-5,5]
p[0].label = '$y = %s$'%sym.latex(y.subs({a:1}))
p[1].label = '$y = %s$'%sym.latex(y.subs({a:2}))
p[0].line_color = 'r'
p[1].line_color = 'g'

p.legend = True
p.show()
```

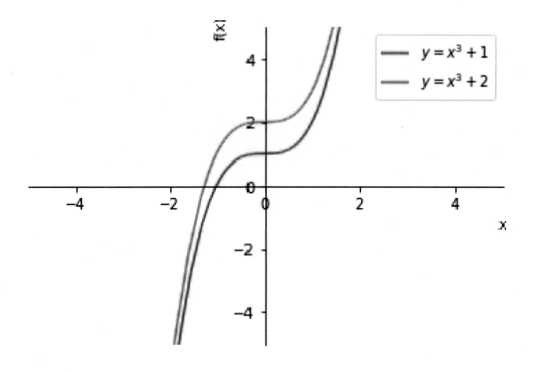

76. Displey two functions $y = a + \dfrac{a^2}{x}$ using sympy library where *a=1* and *a=2*.

```python
import sympy as sym
import sympy.plotting.plot as symplot

x,a = sym.symbols('x,a')

y = (a + a**2/x)

p = symplot(y.subs(a,1),show = False)
p.extend(symplot(y.subs(a,2),show = False))

p.ylim = [-10,10]
p.xlim = [-10,10]
p[0].label = '$y = %s$'%sym.latex(y.subs({a:1}))
p[1].label = '$y = %s$'%sym.latex(y.subs({a:2}))
p[0].line_color = 'r'
p[1].line_color = 'g'

p.legend = True
p.show()
```

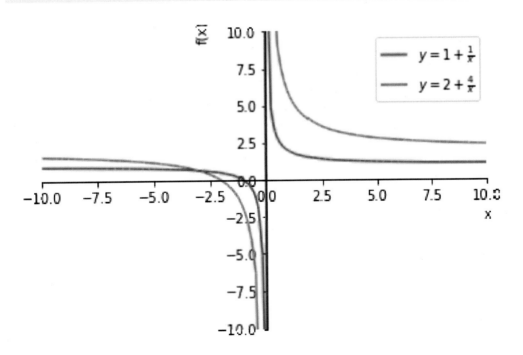

77. Displey all functions $y = \dfrac{2b}{(x^2 - b)}$ **where** $b=\{1, 2, 3, 4\}$.

```python
import sympy as sym
import sympy.plotting.plot as symplot

x,b = sym.symbols('x,b')
color = ['r','g','y','m']

y = (2*b)/((x**2)-b)
p = symplot(y.subs(b,1), show = False)
p[0].label = 'y = $%s$'%sym.latex(2/((x**2)-1))

for i in range(2,5):
    p.extend(symplot(y.subs(b,i), show = False))
    p[i-1].line_color = color[i-1]
    p[i-1].label = 'y = $%s$'%sym.latex(y.subs({b:i}))

p.ylim = [-10,10]
p.xlim = [-5,8]
p.legend = True

p.show()
```

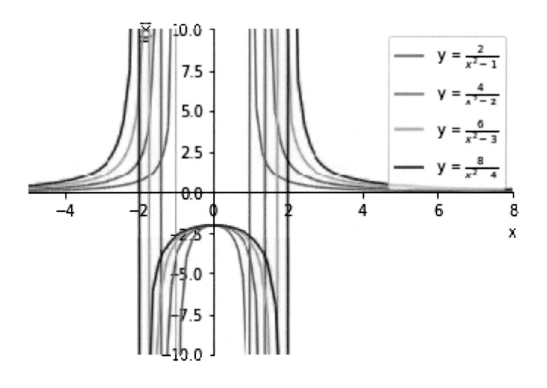

78. Displey all functions of $y = \dfrac{x^2}{b} + 3b$ **where** $b=\{1,2,3\}$.

```python
import sympy as sym
import sympy.plotting.plot as symplot

x,b = sym.symbols('x,b')
color = ['r','g','y','m']

y = (x**2)/b + 3*b
p = symplot(y.subs(b,1), show = False)
p[0].label = 'y = $%s$'%sym.latex((x**2)/1 + 3*1)

for i in range(2,4):
    p.extend(symplot(y.subs(b,i), show = False))
    p[i-1].line_color = color[i-1]
    p[i-1].label = 'y = $%s$'%sym.latex(y.subs({b:i}))

p.ylim = [-20,20]
p.xlim = [-10,15]
p.legend = True

p.show()
```

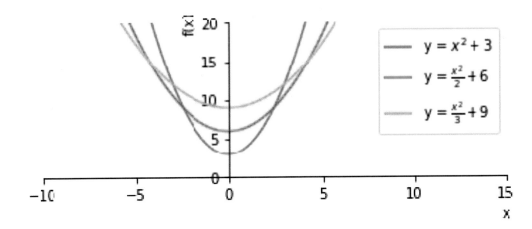

79. Displey all functions of $y=x^2-5b$ **where** $b=\{1, 2, 3, 4\}$**.**

```
import sympy as sym
import sympy.plotting.plot as symplot

x,b = sym.symbols('x,b')
color = ['r','g','y','m']

y = x**2 - 5*b
p = symplot(y.subs(b,1), show = False)
p[0].label = 'y = $%s$'%sym.latex(x**2 - 5*1)

for i in range(2,5):
    p.extend(symplot(y.subs(b,i), show = False))
    p[i-1].line_color = color[i-1]
    p[i-1].label = 'y = $%s$'%sym.latex(y.subs({b:i}))

p.ylim = [-20,20]
p.xlim = [-10,15]
p.legend = True

p.show()
```

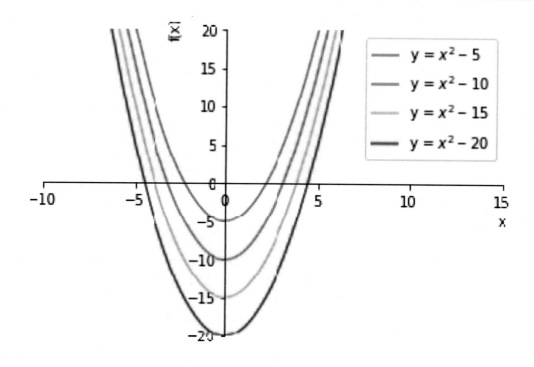

80. Display a matrix $c_{(a, b)} = -1^{a+b}$ **where** $a,b=(0,1,2,3...10)$

```python
import numpy as np
import matplotlib.pyplot as plt

N = 10
A = np.zeros((N,N))

for a in range(0,np.shape(A)[0]):
    for b in range(0, np.shape(A)[1]):
        A[a,b] = (-1)**(a+b)


plt.set_cmap('Greys')
plt.imshow(A)
```

<matplotlib.image.AxesImage at 0x123504710>

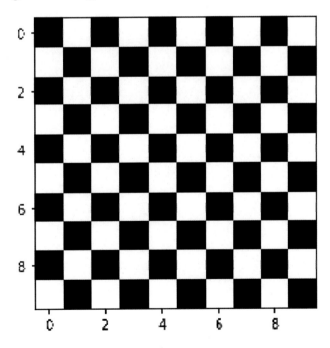

81. Display a matrix $c_{(a,\,b)} = (-1)^a + (-1)^a$ **where** $a,b = (0,1,2,3...19,20)$
You mihgt apply different color scale (cmap).

```python
import numpy as np
import matplotlib.pyplot as plt

N = 20
A = np.zeros((N,N))

for a in range(1,np.shape(A)[0]):
    for b in range(1, np.shape(A)[1]):
        A[a,b] = (-1)**a + (-1)**b


plt.set_cmap('Greys')
plt.imshow(A)
```

<matplotlib.image.AxesImage at 0x12359f3d0>

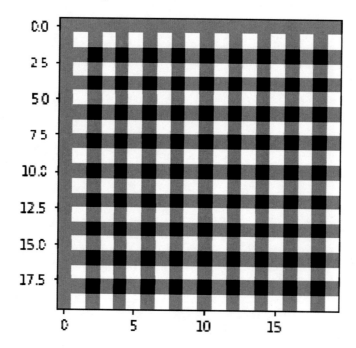

82. Are two fractions equal to each other?

$$\frac{\sum i}{\sum i^2} = \frac{1}{\sum i} \text{ where } i = \{1,2, .. 9,10\}$$

```python
import numpy as np
import matplotlib.pyplot as plt

lst = np.arange(1,11)

exp1 = np.sum(lst)
exp2 = np.sum(lst**2)

ans1 = exp1/exp2
ans2 = 1/exp1

print("The value of both fractions: %s and %s"%(ans1,ans2))

if ans1/ans2 == 1/ans1:
    print("They are equal")
else:
    print("They are NOT equal")
```

The value of both fractions: 0.14285714285714285 and 0.01818181818181818
They are NOT equal

83. Are two fractions equal to each other?

$$\frac{\prod a}{\prod a^2} = \frac{1}{\prod a} \text{ where } i = \{1,2,3,4,5\}$$

```python
import numpy as np
import matplotlib.pyplot as plt

lst = np.arange(1,6)

exp1 = np.prod(lst)
exp2 = np.prod(lst**2)

ans1 = exp1/exp2
ans2 = 1/exp1

print("The value of both fractions: %s and %s"%(ans1,ans2))
```

The value of both fractions: 0.008333333333333333 and 0.008333333333333333

84. Displey the function $y=x^2-1$ and derevative of same function.

```python
import numpy as np
import matplotlib.pyplot as plt


x = np.linspace(-2,2,101)
f = x**2 - 1
df = np.diff(f)

plt.plot(x,f, label = 'f')
plt.plot(x[0:-1],df,'r', label = 'df')

plt.legend()
plt.grid()
plt.axis([-2,2,-1,2])
plt.show()
```

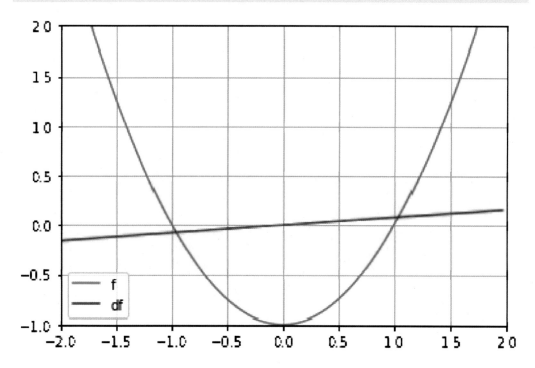

85. Displey the function $y=x^3$ and derevative of same function.

```python
import numpy as np
import matplotlib.pyplot as plt


x = np.linspace(-5,5,101)
f = (x**3)
df = np.diff(f)

plt.plot(x,f, label = 'f')
plt.plot(x[0:-1],df,'r', label = 'df')

plt.plot([-5,5],[0,0],'k--')
plt.plot([0,0],[-5,5],'k--')

plt.legend()
plt.grid()
plt.axis([-5,5,-5,5])
plt.show()
```

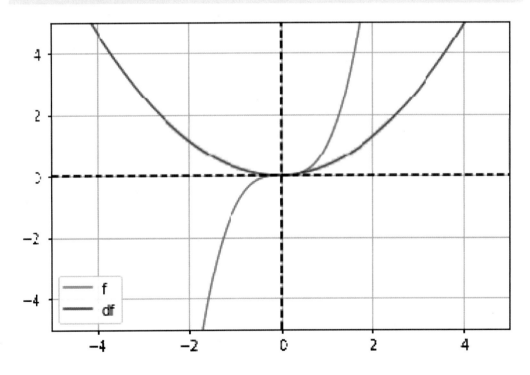

86. Displey the function $y=|-x|^3+2x^2$ **and derevative of same function.**

```python
import numpy as np
import matplotlib.pyplot as plt

x = np.linspace(-5,5,101)
f = np.abs(-x)**3 + 2*x**2
df = np.diff(f)

plt.plot(x,f, label = 'f')
plt.plot(x[0:-1],df,'r', label = 'df')

plt.plot([-5,5],[0,0],'k--')
plt.plot([0,0],[-5,5],'k--')

plt.legend()
plt.grid()
plt.axis([-5,5,-5,5])
plt.show()
```

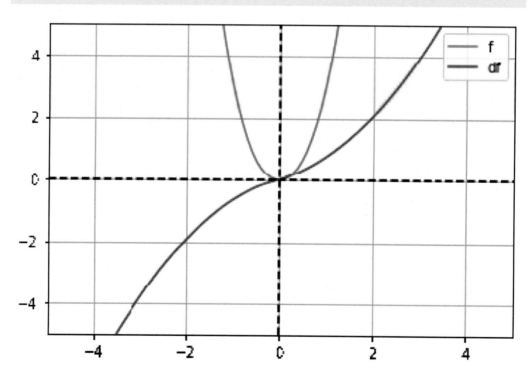

87. Display $z_1 = -2 + i$ and $z_2 = 3 + i$ and display $z_1 + z_2$

```python
import numpy as np
import matplotlib.pyplot as plt

z1 = np.complex(-2, 1)
z2 = np.complex(3, 1)

z1plusz2 = z1+z2

plt.plot([0,np.real(z1)],[0,np.imag(z1)],label = 'z1')
plt.plot([0,np.real(z2)],[0,np.imag(z2)],label = 'z2')
plt.plot([0,np.real(z1plusz2)],[0,np.imag(z1plusz2)],
                                      label = 'z1+z2')


plt.grid()
plt.axis('square')
plt.axis([-5,5,-5,5])
plt.xlabel('real')
plt.ylabel('imag')
plt.legend()

plt.show()
```

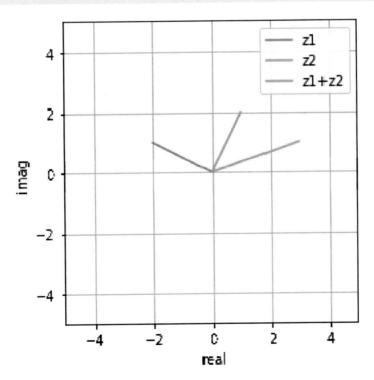

88. Display $t_1=4+i$ **and** $t_2=-2+i$ **and display** t_1+t_2

```python
import numpy as np
import matplotlib.pyplot as plt
import sympy as sym

t1 = np.complex(4, 1)
t2 = np.complex(-2, 1)

t1plust2 = t1+t2

plt.plot([0,np.real(t1)],[0,np.imag(t1)],
        label = 't1 = %s'%sym.latex(t1))
plt.plot([0,np.real(t2)],[0,np.imag(t2)],
        label = 't2 = %s'%sym.latex(t2))
plt.plot([0,np.real(t1plust2)],[0,np.imag(t1plust2)],
        label = 't1+t2 = %s'
        %sym.latex(t1plust2))

plt.grid()
plt.axis('square')
plt.axis([-5,5,-5,5])
plt.xlabel('real')
plt.ylabel('imag')
plt.legend()

plt.show()
```

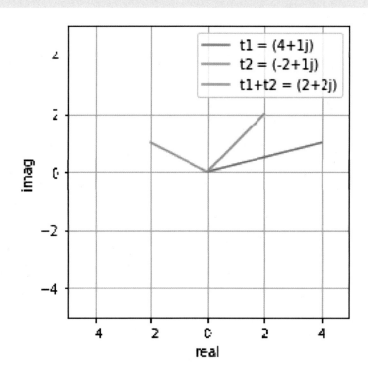

89. Display $z_1 = -3+i$ **and** $z_2 = 4+i$ **and display** $z_1 \times z_2$

```python
import numpy as np
import matplotlib.pyplot as plt
import sympy as sym

z1 = np.complex(-2, 1)
z2 = np.complex(4, 1)

z1timesz2 = z1*z2

plt.plot([0,np.real(z1)],[0,np.imag(z1)],
         label = 'z1 = %s'%sym.latex(z1))
plt.plot([0,np.real(z2)],[0,np.imag(z2)],
         label = 'z2 = %s'%sym.latex(z2))
plt.plot([0,np.real(z1timesz2)],[0,np.imag(z1timesz2)],
         label = 'z1*z2 = %s'
         %sym.latex(z1timesz2))

plt.grid()
plt.axis('square')
plt.axis([-5,5,-5,5])
plt.xlabel('real')
plt.ylabel('imag')
plt.legend()

plt.show()
```

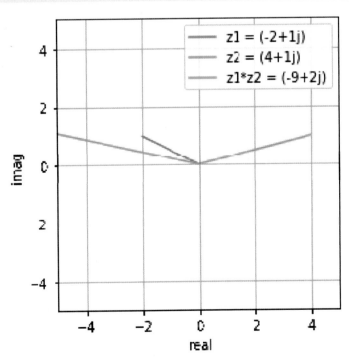

90. Display $k_1 = 1+i$ **and** $k_2 = -2+i$ **and display** $k_1 \times k_2$

```python
import numpy as np
import matplotlib.pyplot as plt
import sympy as sym

k1 = np.complex(1, 1)
k2 = np.complex(-2, 1)

k1timesk2 = k1*k2

plt.plot([0,np.real(k1)],[0,np.imag(k1)],
         label = 'z1 = %s'%sym.latex(k1))
plt.plot([0,np.real(k2)],[0,np.imag(k2)],
         label = 'z2 = %s'%sym.latex(k2))
plt.plot([0,np.real(k1timesk2)],[0,np.imag(k1timesk2)],
         label = 'k1*k2 = %s'
         %sym.latex(k1timesk2))

plt.grid()
plt.axis('square')
plt.axis([-5,5,-5,5])
plt.xlabel('real')
plt.ylabel('imag')
plt.legend()

plt.show()
```

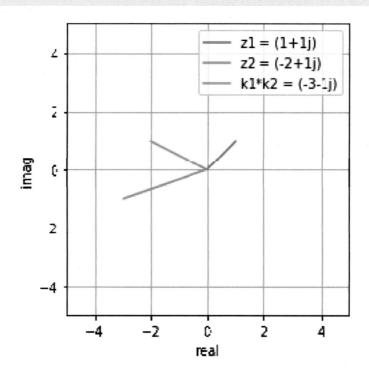

91. Display a circle with a one unit (*2pi*)

```python
import numpy as np
import matplotlib.pyplot as plt

x = np.linspace(0,2*np.pi,100)

plt.plot(np.cos(x),np.sin(x),'r')
plt.plot([-1.5,1.5],[0,0],'--',color=[0.8 , 0.8 , 0.8 , 0.8])
plt.plot([0,0],[-1.5,1.5],'--',color=[0.8 , 0.8 , 0.8 , 0.8])

angle = np.pi/4
plt.plot([0,np.cos(angle) ],[0,np.sin(angle)],'b' )

plt.axis('square')
plt.xlabel('cos(x)')
plt.ylabel('sin(x)')
plt.axis([-1.5 , 1.5 , -1.5 , 1.5])

plt.show()
```

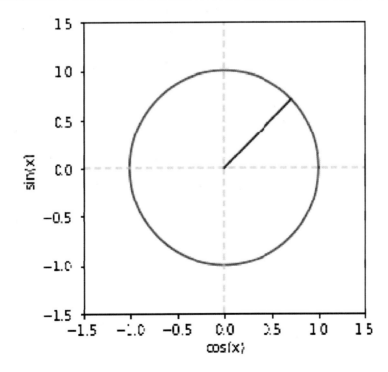

92. Display a HALF of circle with a one unit (*2pi*)

```python
import numpy as np
import matplotlib.pyplot as plt

x = np.linspace(0,1*np.pi,100)

plt.plot(np.cos(x),np.sin(x),'r')
angle = np.pi/4
plt.plot([-1,1 ],[0,0],'r' )

plt.plot([-1.5,1.5],[0,0],'--',color=[0.8 , 0.8 , 0.8 , 0.8])
plt.plot([0,0],[-1.5,1.5],'--',color=[0.8 , 0.8 , 0.8 , 0.8])


plt.axis('square')
plt.xlabel('cos(x)')
plt.ylabel('sin(x)')
plt.axis([-1.5 , 1.5 , -1.5 , 1.5])

plt.show()
```

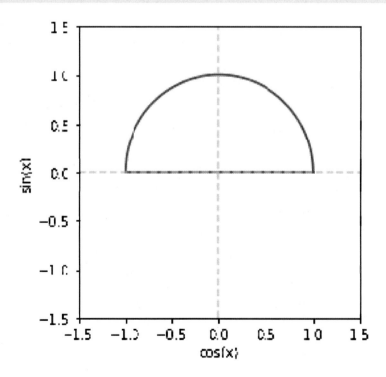

93. Display $k=e^{a}$ **where** $a=(-3, 1.83)$

```
import numpy as np
import matplotlib.pyplot as plt

a = np.linspace(-3,1.83,50)
k = np.exp(a)

for i in k:
    plt.plot([0,np.cos(i)],[0,np.sin(i)])

plt.axis('square')
plt.axis('off')

plt.show()
```

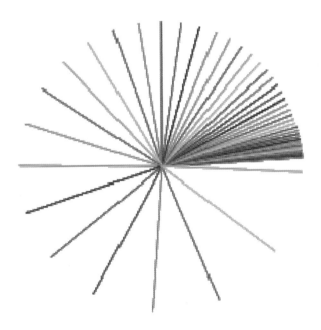

94. Display *y=log(x).*

```
import numpy as num
import matplotlib.pyplot as plt

x = np.linspace(-3,3,99)

plt.plot(x,np.log(x))
plt.xlabel('x')
plt.ylabel('$log(x)$')

plt.show()
```

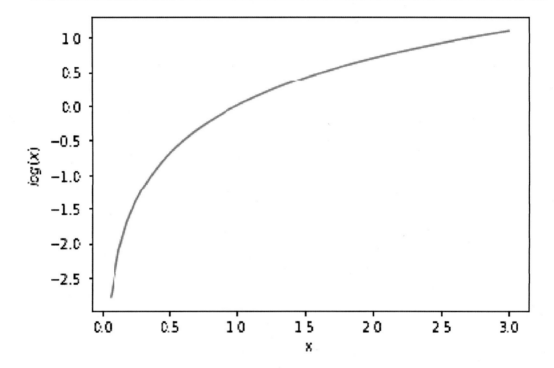

95. Plot y_1 **and** y_2**.** $y_1=log(e^x)$, $y_2=e^{log(x)}$. $x=(0.0001, 10)$

```python
import numpy as np
import matplotlib.pyplot as plt

x = np.linspace(0.0001, 10, 10)

y1 = np.log(np.exp(x))
y2 = np.exp(np.log(x))

plt.plot(x,y1,label = '$\\log(e^x)$')
plt.plot(x,y2,'ro', label = '$e^{\\log(x)}$')

plt.legend()
plt.axis('square')


plt.show()
```

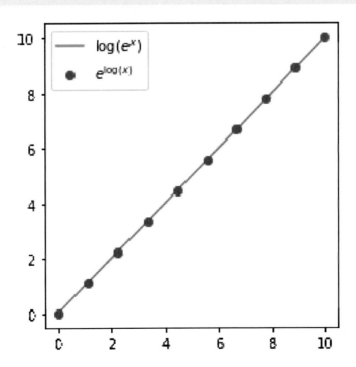

96. **Displey $z^a=1$ where z is a complex number.**

$$z = e^{\frac{2\pi i n}{a}} \text{ where } n=0,1,2, ..., a-1$$

```python
import numpy as np
import matplotlib.pyplot as plt
import sympy as sym
from IPython.display import display, Math

a = 5
for n in range(0,a):
    b = sym.exp(2*sym.pi*sym.I*n/a)
    c = np.exp(2*np.pi*1j*n/a)
    display(Math('(%s)^%s \\Rightarrow %s'
                %(sym.latex(b),n,sym.latex(b**a))))
    plt.plot([0,np.real(c)],[0,np.imag(c)])

angle = np.linspace(0,2*np.pi,100)
plt.plot(np.cos(angle),np.sin(angle),color='gray')

plt.axis('square')
plt.show()
```

$$(1)^0 \Rightarrow 1$$

$$\left(e^{\frac{2i\pi}{5}}\right)^1 \Rightarrow 1$$

$$\left(e^{\frac{4i\pi}{5}}\right)^2 \Rightarrow 1$$

$$\left(e^{\frac{6i\pi}{5}}\right)^3 \Rightarrow 1$$

$$\left(e^{\frac{8i\pi}{5}}\right)^4 \Rightarrow 1$$

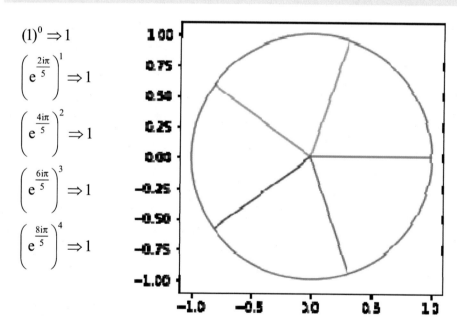

97. Displey $z^a=1$ **where z is a complex number.**

$$z = ne^{\frac{2\pi in}{a}} \text{ where } n=0,1,2,\ ...,\ a-1$$

```python
import numpy as np
import matplotlib.pyplot as plt
import sympy as sym
from IPython.display import display, Math

a = 250
for n in range(0,a):
    b = n*sym.exp(2*sym.pi*sym.I*n/a)
    c = n*np.exp(2*np.pi*1j*n/a)
    # Optional:
    #display(Math('(%s)^{%s} \\Rightarrow
%s'%(sym.latex(b),n,sym.latex(b**a))))
    plt.plot([0,np.real(c)],[0,np.imag(c)])

angle = np.linspace(0,2*np.pi,100)
plt.plot(np.cos(angle),np.sin(angle),color='gray')

plt.axis('square')
plt.xlim(-150,250)
plt.ylim(-250,150)
plt.show()
```

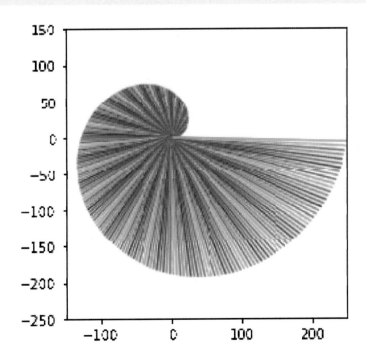

98. Display a LINEAR SCALE and LOGARITHMIC SCALE that has same boundaries and approach each other.

```python
import numpy as num
import matplotlib.pyplot as plt

min_value = 1
max_value = 200
n = 50

linear = np.linspace(min_value, max_value, n)
logarithmic = np.logspace(np.log10(min_value),
np.log10(max_value),n)

plt.plot(linear,linear, label = "Linear Scale")
plt.plot(linear,logarithmic, label = "Logarithmic Scale")

plt.legend()
plt.axis('Square')

plt.show()
```

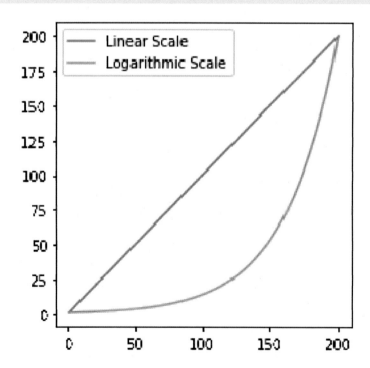

99. **Calculate and illustrate the following expressions (which ones are same expressions?)**

$log(5 \times 4)$

$log(5) \times log(4)$

$log(5) + log(4)$

```python
import numpy as num
from IPython.display import display, Math

a = 5
b = 4

exp1 = np.log(a*b)
exp2 = np.log(a) * np.log(b)
exp3 = np.log(a) + np.log(b)

display(Math('\\log(%s \\times %s) = %s'
            %(a,b,exp1)))
display(Math('\\log(%s) \\times log(%s) = %s'
            %(a,b,exp2)))
display(Math('\\log(%s) + log(%s) = %s'
            %(a,b,exp3)))
display(Math('\\log(%s \\times %s) = \\log(%s) + log(%s)'
            %(a,b,a,b)))
display(Math('\\log(%s \\times %s) \\neq \\log(%s) \\times log(%s)'
            %(a,b,a,b)))
```

$log(5 \times 4) = 2.995732273553991$
$log(5) \times log(4) = 2.2311547025799614$
$log(5) + log(4) = 2.995732273553991$
$log(5 \times 4) = log(5) + log(4)$
$log(5 \times 4) \neq log(5) \times log(4)$

100. **Illustrate the proof of following equation:**
$log(a^b) = b \times log(a)$ where $a = 3$ and $b = 6$.

```python
import numpy as num

a = 3
b = 6

exp1 = np.log(a**b)
exp2 = b * np.log(a)
# if the value of both expressions are same, so the
difference must be zero

print(exp1 - exp2)
```

0.0

PHYSICS

Python Solutions
for
100 Physics Questions

1. **Display Mr. Williams left Vancouver with his car at 4pm and reached Kamloops at 7:30 pm. If Mr. Williams travels with average velocity of 70 km/h, what is the distance from Vancouver to Kamloops?**

$$v = \frac{\Delta x}{\Delta t}$$

Since

$$\Delta t = 7:30\ PM - 4:00\ PM = 3.5\ hours$$

$$70 = \frac{\Delta x}{3.5}$$

$$\Delta x = 245 km$$

```
dt = 7.5 - 4     # difference in time 7:30 - 4:00
v = 70   # velocity

# since v = dx/dt, so   dx = v(dt)

dx = dt*v
print(dx)
```

245.0

2. Mr. Hamilton travels from Seattle to California, and total distance is roughly 900 mi. Mr. Hamilton drove 400 mi with average velocity of 50 mph in his very first day. Second day, He traveled 300 mi with average velocity of 60 mph. In his third day, He drove 200 mi with average velocity of 40 mph. What is his average velocity during his trip?

$$x_{total} = x_1 + x_2 + x_3 = 400 + 300 + 200$$

$$x_{total} = 900 \ mi$$

$$t_{total} = t_1 + t_2 + t_3$$

$$t_{total} = \frac{x_1}{v_1} + \frac{x_2}{v_2} + \frac{x_3}{v_3}$$

$$t_{total} = \frac{400}{50} + \frac{300}{60} + \frac{200}{40}$$

$$t_{total} = 18 \ hours$$

$$v_{average} = \frac{x_{total}}{t_{total}}$$

$$v_{average} = \frac{900}{18}$$

$$v_{average} = 50 \ mph$$

```
x1 = 400
x2 = 300
x3 = 200

t1 = 50
t2 = 60
t3 = 40

x_total = x1 + x2 + x3
t_total = x1/t1 + x2/t2 + x3/t3

v_average = x_total/t_total

print(v_average)
```

50.0

3. **Mr. Smith leaves his classroom and walks to the right with a constant speed of 5 m/s for 6s. Then he slowed down in 2s and stoped. What is his displacement?**

$v_1 = 5\,m/s$

$t_1 = 6\,s$

He starts to slow down when his velocity is 5 m/s so;

$v_i = 5\,m/s$

$v_f = 0\,m/s$

$t_2 = 2\,s$

$\Delta x = ?$

$x_1 = v_1 \cdot t_1$

$x_1 = 5 \cdot 6$

$x_1 = 30\,m$

$x_2 = \dfrac{\left(v_i + v_f\right)}{2} \cdot t_2$

$x_2 = \dfrac{(5 + 0)}{2} \cdot 2$

$x_2 = 5\,m$

$\Delta x = x_1 + x_2$

$\Delta x = 30 + 5$

$\Delta x = 35\,m$

```
v_1 = 5
t_1 = 6
v_i = 5
v_f = 0
t_2 = 2

x_1 = v_1 * t_1

x_2 = ((v_i + v_f)/2)*t_2

dx = x_1 + x_2

print("The displacement is",dx,"m")
```

The displacement is 35.0 m

4. **Two friends are racing to reach 5th floor of the building. First man gets on the elevator, and elevator accelerates up with an acceleration of 2 m/s². Second man climbs the stairs with constant velocity of 10 m/s. If the height of one floor is 3 m, who reaches the 5th floor first?**

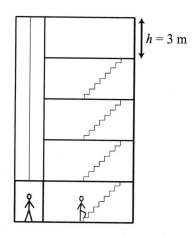

$h = 3$ m

We have to compare t_1 and t_2

Height of building till 5th floor $= 3 \times 4 = 12\,m$

We multiply with 4 because the displacement is from the bottom of the first floor to the top of the 4th floor

$$h = \frac{1}{2}at^2$$

$$12 = \frac{1}{2}2\left(t_1\right)^2$$

$$t_1 = \sqrt{12} = 3.46\,s$$

$$t_2 = \frac{x}{v_2}$$

$$t_2 = \frac{12}{10} = 1.2\,s$$

Then, since $t_1 > t_2$, Second man who climb the stairs will reach faster

```python
import math

building_height = 4*3
acceleration = 2

# From the formula   h = (1/2) * a * t**2
# 12 = (1/2) * 2 * t1**2

t1 = math.sqrt(12)

v2 = 10
t2 = 12/10

if t1>t2:
    print("The second man will reach faster")
else:
    print("The first man will reach to 5th floor faster")
```

The second man who climbs the stairs will reach faster

5. **A school bus starts to its trip from point S. First it picks up Anh from point A, then drives 150 m towards north and picks up Bobby from point B. At last it drives west for 200 m and picks up Chris from point C. What is the total distance that the bus traveled from point S to C? What is its displacement from point S to C?**

$D_{S \text{ to } A} = 200 \text{ m}$
$D_{A \text{ to } B} = 150 \text{ m}$
$D_{B \text{ to } C} = 200 \text{ m}$
$D_{total} = D_{S \text{ to } A} + D_{A \text{ to } B} + D_{B \text{ to } C}$
$D_{total} = 200+150+200$
$D_{total} = 550 \text{ m}$
$X_{initial} = 0 \text{ m}$
$X_{final} = 150 \text{ m}$
$\Delta x = X_{final} - X_{initial}$
$\Delta x = 150 - 0$
$\Delta x = 150 \text{ m}$

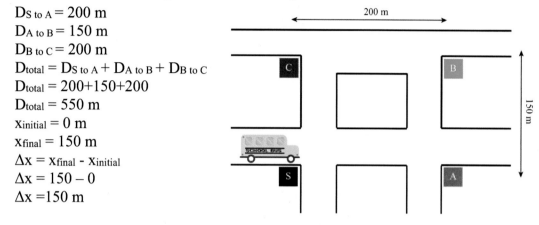

```
D_SA = 200
D_AB = 150
D_BC = 200
D_total = D_SA + D_AB + D_BC

X_initial = 150
X_final = 0
Dx = X_initial - X_final

print("Total disance is", D_total)
print("The displacement from point S to C is", Dx)
```

Total disance is 550
The displacement from point S to C is 150

6. A jet aircraft has 3 seconds and 450 m of runway to take off from an aircraft carrier ship. If it starts from rest, what is the average acceleration of the jet aircraft?

$\Delta x = 450 \, m$

$t = 3 \, s$

$v_i = 0 \, m/s$

$a = ?$

$\Delta x = v_i \cdot t + \dfrac{1}{2} a t^2$

$a = \dfrac{2\left(\Delta x - v_i \cdot t\right)}{t^2}$

$a = \dfrac{2(450 - 0 \cdot 3)}{3^2}$

$a = 100 \, m/s^2$

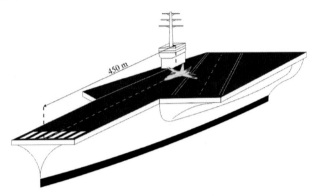

```
dx = 450
t = 3
vi = 0

# formula: dx = v * t + (1/2) * a * t**2

a = (2*(dx-vi*t))/(t**2)
print("The average acceleration of the jet aircraft = ",
      int(a),"m/s^2" )
```

The average acceleration of the jet aircraft = 100m/s^2

7. **NHRA hosts drag races where cars require parachutes to stop if the max speed is 325 km/h. A car deploys its parachute when its velocity is 400 m/s. If the deceleration of the car is 25 m/s², how long does it take for the car to stop completely?**

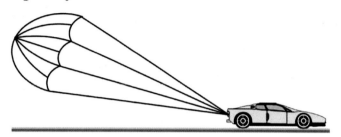

$v_i = 400 \, m/s$

$v_f = 0 \, m/s$

$a = -25 \, m/s^2$

$t = ?$

$v_f = v_i + a \cdot t$

$t = \dfrac{v_f - v_i}{a}$

$t = \dfrac{0 - 400}{-25}$

$t = 16 \, s$

```
vi = 400
vf = 0
a = -25

# formula: vf = vi + a*t

t = (vf - vi)/(a)
print("It will take",int(t),
      "seconds for the car to stop completely")
```

It will take 16 seconds for the car to stop completely

8. Alex pushes a ball down on an incline. At the moment the ball leaves Alex's hand, velocity of the ball is 2.6 m/s. If the acceleration of the ball down the ramp is constant and equal to 3.1 m/s² what is going to be the velocity of the ball at the end of the ramp? Length of the incline is 12.4 m.

$v_i = 2.6 \, m/s$

$a = 3.1 \, m/s^2$

$\Delta x = 12.4 \, m$

$v_f = ?$

$$\left(v_f\right)^2 = \left(v_i\right)^2 + 2a \cdot \Delta x$$

$$v_f = \sqrt{\left(v_i\right)^2 + 2a \cdot \Delta x}$$

$$v_f = \sqrt{2.6^2 + 2 \cdot 3.1 \cdot 12.4}$$

$$v_f = 9.15 \, m/s$$

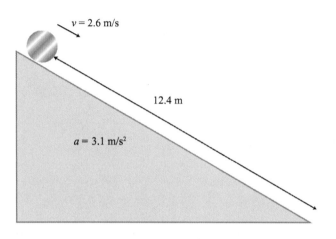

```
import math
vi = 2.6
a = 3.1
dx = 12.4

# Formula: vf**2 = vi**2 + 2 * a * dx

vf = math.sqrt(vi**2 + 2*a*dx)
print("The velocity of the ball is",
      round(vf,2),"m/s")
```

The velocity of the ball at the end of the ramp is 9.15 m/s

9. **The graph below shows the velocity-time graph of an object. What is the displacement of the object?**

$v_i = 10 \, m/s$

$v_f = 30 \, m/s$

$t = 4s$

$\Delta x = ?$

$$\Delta x = t \cdot \left(\frac{v_i + v_f}{2} \right)$$

$$\Delta x = 4 \cdot \left(\frac{10 + 30}{2} \right)$$

$\Delta x = 80 \, m$

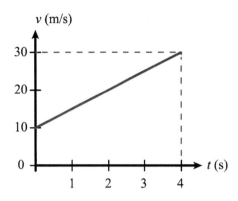

```
vi = 10
vf = 30
t = 4

dx = t * ((vi + vf)/(2))
print("The is the displacement of the object is",int(dx),"m")
```

The is the displacement of the object is 80m.

10. An average rain cloud is 18,288 m above the ground. What will be the speed of the rain droplets when they hit the ground, if there were no air resistance? Assume that initial speed of the rain is 0 m/s.

$$\Delta x = 18,288 \, m, \ v_i = 0 \, m/s$$

$$a = 10 \, m/s^2, \ t = ?$$

$$\Delta x = v_i \cdot t + \frac{1}{2} at^2$$

$$t = \sqrt{2 \cdot \Delta x \cdot a}, \ t = \sqrt{2 \cdot 18,288 \cdot 10}, \ t = 605 \, s$$

$$v_f = v_i + a \cdot t, \ v_f = 0 + 10 \cdot 605, \ v_f = 6,050 \, m/s$$

$h = 18,288 \, m$

```python
import math

dx = 18288
vi = 0
a = 10

# Formula: dx = vi * t + (1/2) * a * t**2

t = math.sqrt(2*dx*a)

vf = vi + (a*(round(t)))
print("The speed of the rain will be",
      int(vf),"m/s")
```

The speed of the rain droplets when they hit the ground is 6050 m/s

11. Find the x component of vector A.

$A = 24$

$\theta = 40°$

$A_x = ?$

$A_x = A \cdot \cos \theta$

$A_x = 24 \cdot \cos 40$

$A_x = 24 \cdot 0.766$

$A_x = 18.39$

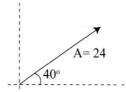

```
import math

A = 24
angle = 40

ax = A * round(math.cos(math.radians(angle)),2)
print("The x component of vector A is",ax)
```

The x component of vector A is 18.48

12. What is the length of the resultant vector of B+C?

$B_x = B \cdot \cos 73, \; B_x = 18 \cdot 0.29, \; B_x = 5.22$

$B_y = B \cdot \sin 73, \; B_y = 18 \cdot 0.96, \; B_y = 17.28$

$C_x = C \cdot \cos(270 - 50), \; C_x = 10 \cdot -0.77, \; C_x = -7.70$

$C_y = C \cdot \sin(270 - 50), \; C_y = 10 \cdot -0.64, \; C_y = -6.40$

$$R = \sqrt{\left(B_x + C_x\right)^2 + \left(B_y + C_y\right)^2}$$

$$R = \sqrt{\left(5.22 + (-7.70)\right)^2 + \left(17.28 + (-6.40)\right)^2}$$

$R = 11.16$

```python
import math

B = 18
C = 10
angle_1 = 73
angle_2 = 50

Bx =  B * round(math.cos(math.radians(angle_1)),2)
By = B * round(math.sin(math.radians(angle_1)),2)

Cx =  C * round(math.cos(math.radians(270 - angle_2)),2)
Cy = C * round(math.sin(math.radians(270 - angle_2)),2)

R = round(math.sqrt((Bx + Cx)**2 + (By + Cy)**2),2)

print("The length of the resultant vecor or B + C is",R)
```

The length of the resultant vecor or B + C is 11.16

13. John hits to a ball with a horizontal velocity of 200 m/s from a cliff. If the height of the cliff is 45 m, what is the range of the ball?

$$v_{x,i} = 200 \, m/s, \ v_{y,i} = 0 \, m/s$$

$$a_x = 0 \, m/s^2, \quad a_y = 10 \, m/s^2$$

$$\Delta y = 45 \, m, \qquad t = \, ?$$

$$\Delta y = v_{y,i} \cdot t + \frac{1}{2} a_y \cdot t^2$$

$$\Delta y = 0 \cdot t + \frac{1}{2} a_y \cdot t^2$$

$$t = \sqrt{\frac{2 \cdot \Delta y}{a_y}}, \ t = \sqrt{\frac{2 \cdot 45}{10}}$$

$$t = 3 \, s$$

$$\Delta x = v_{x,i} \cdot t + \frac{1}{2} a_x \cdot t^2, \ \Delta x = 200 \cdot 3 + \frac{1}{2} 0 \cdot 3^2, \ \Delta x = 600 \, m$$

$v = 200$ m/s

$h = 45$ m

$R = ?$

```python
import math

vxi = 200
vyi = 0
ax = 0
ay = 10
dy = 45

# Formula: dy = vyi * t + (1/2) * ay * t**2

t = math.sqrt((2*dy)/(ay))

dx = vxi * t + (1/2) * ax * t**2

print("The range of the ball is", round(dx),"m")
```

The range of the ball is 600 m

14. A soccer player is hitting to a ball with an initial speed of 50 m/s and initial angle of 53 with respect to the horizontal axis. What is the distance the ball is going to hit to ground first?

$v_i = 50\, m/s, \quad \theta = 53°$

$a_x = 0\, m/s^2, \quad a_y = -10\, m/s^2$

$\Delta y = 0, \quad \Delta x = ?$

$v_{x,i} = v_i \cdot \cos 53,$

$v_{x,i} = 50 \cdot 0.6, \quad v_{x,i} = 30\, m/s$

$v_{y,i} = v_i \cdot \sin 53,$

$v_{y,i} = 50 \cdot 0.8, \quad v_{y,i} = 40\, m/s$

$v_{y,f} = -40\, m/s, \quad v_{y,f} = v_{y,i} + a \cdot t$

$t = \dfrac{v_{y,f} - v_{y,i}}{a_y}, \quad t = \dfrac{-40 - (40)}{-10}, \quad t = 8\, s$

$\Delta x = v_{x,i} \cdot t + \dfrac{1}{2} a_x \cdot t^2, \quad \Delta x = 30 \cdot 8 + \dfrac{1}{2} 0 \cdot 8^2, \quad \Delta x = 240\, m$

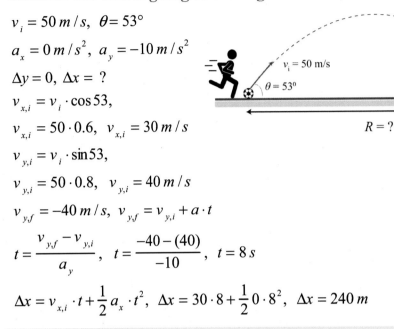

```
import math

vi = 50
angle = 53
ax = 0
ay = -10

# dy = ? and dx = ?

vxi = vi * round(math.cos(math.radians(angle)),2)

vyi = vi * round(math.sin(math.radians(angle)),2)

vyf = -vyi

# Formula: vyf = vyi + a*t

t = (vyf - vyi)/(ay)

dx = vxi * t + (1/2)*ax * t**2
print("The distance is",int(dx),"m.")
```

The distance teh ball is going to hit to ground first is 240 m.

15. A marble is rolling on a flat frictionless table top with a speed of 15 m/s as shown in the figure below. It rolls on the table then starts to fall. What is the time in the air for the marble right before it hits the floor for the first time?

$v_{x,i} = 15\,m/s,\ v_{y,i} = 0\,m/s$

$a_x = 0\,m/s^2,\ a_y = 10\,m/s^2$

$\Delta y = 5\,m,\qquad t = ?$

$\Delta y = v_{y,i} \cdot t + \dfrac{1}{2}\,a_y \cdot t^2$

$\Delta y = 0 \cdot t + \dfrac{1}{2}\,a_y \cdot t^2$

$t = \sqrt{\dfrac{2 \cdot \Delta y}{a_y}},\ t = \sqrt{\dfrac{2 \cdot 5}{10}},\ t = 1\,s$

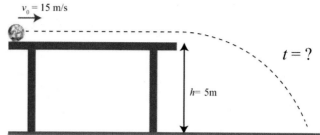

```
import math

vxi = 15
vyi = 0
ax = 0
ay = 10
dy = 5

# t = ?
# Fromula: dy = vyi*t + (1/2)*ay*t

t = math.sqrt((2*dy)/(ay))
print("the time for marble is",
      int(t),"second.")
```

The time for marble is 1 second.

16. Velocity of a boat at a still water is 8 m/s. But it is going to travel in a river where the velocity of current is 6 m/s. The width of the river is 40 m. How far away is the boat going be dragged by the current if it heads straight across the river? (Assume velocities are constant)

$L = 40m, \ v_{boat} = 8m/s,$

$v_{river} = 6m/s, \quad \Delta x = ?$

$\Delta y = v_y \cdot t$

$t = \dfrac{L}{v_{boat}}, \ t = \dfrac{40}{8}, \ t = 5s$

$\Delta x = v_{river} \cdot t, \ \Delta x = 6 \cdot 5, \ \Delta x = 30m$

$x = ?$

$v_{river} = 6 \text{ m/s}$

$L = 40 \text{ m}$

$v_{boat} = 8 \text{ m/s}$

```
L = 40
v_boat = 8
v_river = 6

# Formula: dy = vy * t

t = L/v_boat

dx = v_river * t
print("Distance = ",int(dx),"m")
```

Distance = 30 m

17. Car A is going with a velocity of 30 m/s toward East and car B is going towards North with a velocity of 40 m/s. What is the relative velocity of car A with respect to car B.

$v_{observer}$ = 40 m/s towards Noth

$v_{observed}$ = 30 m/s towards East

$v_{Relative}$ =?

$v_{Relative} = v_{observed} - v_{observer}$

Since two velocities are in different axis, operation is going to be vector operation

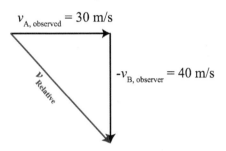

$$v_{Relative} = \sqrt{\left(v_{observed}\right)^2 + \left(-v_{observer}\right)^2}$$

$$v_{Relative} = \sqrt{(40)^2 + (-30)^2}$$

$v_{Relative}$ = 50m/s towards south west

```python
import math

v_north = 40
v_east = 30

v_relative = math.sqrt(v_north**2 + (-v_east)**2)
print("The relative velocity of car A with respect to car B is ",
      int(v_relative),"m/s towards south west")
```

The relative velocity of car A with respect to car B is 50 m/s towards south west.

18. A marble is sliding with a velocity of 2 m/s on a frictionless table. A board is placed 50 cm in front of the table on the way of the marble. Calculate the distance from the floor to the point that the marble is going to hit to board. Height of the table is 1.5 m.

$$v_{x,i} = 2\,m/s, \quad v_{y,i} = 0\,m/s$$

$$a_x = 0\,m/s^2, \quad a_y = 10\,m/s^2$$

$$\Delta x = 50\,cm = 0.5\,m$$

$$h = 1.5\,m, \quad \Delta y = ?, \quad t = ?$$

$$\Delta x = v_{x,i} \cdot t + \frac{1}{2}a_x \cdot t^2,$$

$$\Delta x = v_{x,i} \cdot t + \frac{1}{2} \cdot 0 \cdot t^2$$

$$t = \frac{\Delta x}{v_{x,i}}, \quad t = \frac{0.5}{2}, \quad t = 0.25\,s$$

$$\Delta y = v_{y,i} \cdot t + \frac{1}{2}a_y \cdot t^2, \quad \Delta y = 0 \cdot 0.25 + \frac{1}{2}10 \cdot (0.25)^2$$

$$\Delta y = 0.31\,m, \quad ? = h - \Delta y, \quad ? = 1.50 - 0.31, \quad ? = 1.19\,m$$

```
vxi = 2
vyi = 0
ax = 9
ay = 10
dx = 0.5
h = 1.5

# Formula: dx = vxi * t + (1/2) * ax * t**2

t = dx/vxi

dy = vyi*t + (1/2)*ay*t**2

d = h - dy

print("The distance is",round(d,2),"m")
```

The distance from the floor to the point that the marble is going to hit to board is 1.19 m.

19. A basketball player jumps and throws the ball with an angle of 37° due to horizontal. What should be the velocity of the ball for him to score?

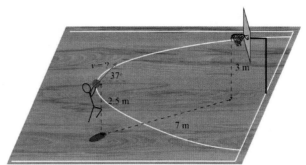

$\Delta x = 7\,m,\ \Delta y = 0.5\,m$

$a_x = 0\,m/s^2,\ a_y = -10\,m/s^2$

$\theta = 37°,\ v_i = ?$

$v_{x,i} = v_i \cdot \cos 37,\ v_{x,i} = v_i \cdot 0.799,\ v_{y,i} = v_i \cdot \sin 37,\ v_{y,i} = v_i \cdot 0.6$

$\Delta x = v_{x,i} \cdot t + \frac{1}{2} a_x \cdot t^2,\ \Delta x = v_{x,i} \cdot t + \frac{1}{2} \cdot 0 \cdot t^2,\ t = \frac{7}{v_i \cdot \cos 37}$

$\Delta y = v_{y,i} \cdot t + \frac{1}{2} a_y \cdot t^2,\ \Delta y = v_i \cdot \sin 37 \cdot \frac{\Delta x}{v_i \cdot \cos 37} + \frac{1}{2} a_y \cdot t^2$

$t = \sqrt{\dfrac{2 \cdot [\Delta y - (\Delta x \cdot \tan 37)]}{a_y}},\ t = \sqrt{\dfrac{2 \cdot [0.5 - (7 \cdot \tan 37)]}{-10}},\ t = 0.977\,s$

$v_i = \dfrac{\Delta x}{t \cdot \cos 37},\ v_i = \dfrac{7}{0.977 \cdot 0.799},\ v_i = 8.97\,m/s$

```
import math

dx = 7
dy = 0.5
ax = 0
ay = -10
angle = 37

vxi = vi * math.cos(math.radians(angle)) # vi = ?
vyi = vi * math.sin(math.radians(angle)) # vi = ?

# Formula: dx = vxi * t + (1/2) * ax * t**2 where ax = 0

t = dx / vxi

# Formula: dy = vyi * t + (1/2) * ay * t**2

t = math.sqrt( (2 * (dy-(dx *
math.tan(math.radians(angle)))))/ay )

vi = dx / (t * math.cos(math.radians(angle)))
print("The velocity of the boll should be", round(vi,2),"m/s")
```

The velocity of the boll should be 8.97 m/s

20. A stunt man drives a car off a cliff straight and tries to pass through a fire hoop that is located 300 ahead and 45 m below the edge of the cliff. What should be the velocity of the car?

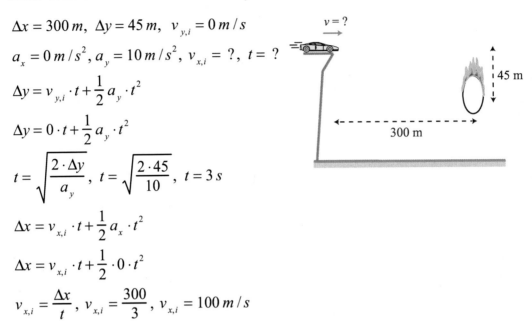

$\Delta x = 300\,m,\ \Delta y = 45\,m,\ v_{y,i} = 0\,m/s$

$a_x = 0\,m/s^2, a_y = 10\,m/s^2, v_{x,i} = ?,\ t = ?$

$\Delta y = v_{y,i} \cdot t + \dfrac{1}{2} a_y \cdot t^2$

$\Delta y = 0 \cdot t + \dfrac{1}{2} a_y \cdot t^2$

$t = \sqrt{\dfrac{2 \cdot \Delta y}{a_y}},\ t = \sqrt{\dfrac{2 \cdot 45}{10}},\ t = 3\,s$

$\Delta x = v_{x,i} \cdot t + \dfrac{1}{2} a_x \cdot t^2$

$\Delta x = v_{x,i} \cdot t + \dfrac{1}{2} \cdot 0 \cdot t^2$

$v_{x,i} = \dfrac{\Delta x}{t},\ v_{x,i} = \dfrac{300}{3},\ v_{x,i} = 100\,m/s$

```python
import math

dx = 300
dy = 45
vyi = 0
ax = 0
ay = 10

# Formula: dy = vyi * t + (1/2) * a * t**2 where vyi = 0

t = math.sqrt((2*dy)/ay)

# Formula: dx = vxi * t + (1/2) * ax * t**2 where ax = 0

vxi = dx/t

print("The velocity of the car should be",round(vxi),"m/s")
```

The velocity of the car should be 100 m/s.

21. A horse is pulling a cart with an acceleration of 2 m/s². The horse is 450 kg, and the cart is 400 kg, then what is the tension on the rope which ties the horse and the cart?

$$m_{sys} = 450 + 400 = 850 \, kg$$

$$a_{horse} = a_{sys} = 2 \, m/s^2$$

$$F_{sys} = m_{sys} a_{sys}$$

$$F_{sys} = 850 \cdot 2$$

$$F_{sys} = 1700 \, N$$

$$F_{sys} - T = m_{horse} a_{horse}$$

$$T = F_{sys} - m_{horse} a_{horse}$$

$$T = 1700 - 450 \cdot 2$$

$$T = 800 \, N$$

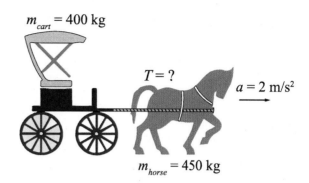

$m_{cart} = 400$ kg

$T = ?$

$a = 2$ m/s²

$m_{horse} = 450$ kg

```
m_sys = 450 + 400
a_sys = 2
m_horse = 450

F_sys = m_sys * a_sys

# Formula: F_sys - T = m_horse * a_horse

T = F_sys - m_horse * a_sys
print("The tension of the rope is", T,"N")
```

The tension of the rope is 800 N

22. A box is pushed by horizontal force 50 N on a smooth surface, and the weight of box is 20 N, what is the acceleration of the system?

$F = 50\,N$

$W = 20\,N$

$a = ?$

$W = mg$

$m = \dfrac{W}{g} = \dfrac{20}{2} = 2\,kg$

$\Sigma F = ma$

$a = \dfrac{\Sigma F}{m} = \dfrac{50}{2}$

$a = 25\,m/s^2$

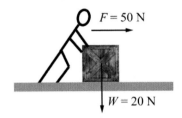

$F = 50\,N$

$W = 20\,N$

```
F = 50
W = 20
g = 10

# Formula: W = m*g

m = W/g

# Formula: F = m*a

a = F/m

print("The acceleration of the system is",
      round(a),"m/s^2")
```

The acceleration of the system is 25m/s^2

23. A 2kg of mass box is pulled by 10N of force making an angle of 37º due horizontal in the figure below. If the coefficient of friction in between the box and the surface is 0.5, then what is the acceleration of the system?

$F = 10\,N, \quad \theta = 37°$

$m = 2\,kg, \quad \mu = 0.5, \quad a = ?$

$F_x = F\cos\theta, \quad F_x = 10 \cdot \cos 37, \quad F_x = 8\,N$

$F_y = F\cos\theta, \quad F_y = 10 \cdot \sin 37, \quad F_y = 6\,N$

$F_N = mg - F_y, \quad F_N = (2 \cdot 10) - 6 = 14\,N$

$F_f = F_N \cdot \mu, \quad F_f = 14 \cdot 0.5 = 7\,N$

$\Sigma F = ma, \quad F_x - F_f = ma$

$a = \dfrac{F_x - F_f}{m} = \dfrac{8 - 7}{2}$

$a = 0.5\,m/s^2$

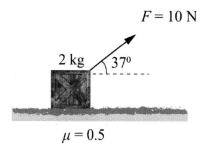

```python
import math
F = 10
angle = 37
m = 2
friction = 0.5
g = 10

Fx = F * math.cos(math.radians(angle))
Fy = F * math.sin(math.radians(angle))

Fn = m*g - Fy
Ff = Fn * friction

# Formula: Total_F = m*a  --> Fx - Ff = m*a

a = (Fx - Ff)/m
print("The acceleration of system is",round(a,1))
```

The acceleration of system is 0.5

24. A man stands on a bathroom scale and the scale measures 750 N. If this man stands on the same scale in an elevator while the elevator is going down with an acceleration of 2.5 m/s², what is the value on the scale?

$W_{man} = 750\,N$

$a = 2.5\,m/s^2$

$F_N = ?$

$W = mg$

$m = \dfrac{W}{g} = \dfrac{750}{10} = 75\,kg$

$\Sigma F = ma$

$W - F_N = ma$

$F_N = W - ma = 750 - (75 \cdot 2.5)$

$F_N = 562.5\,N$

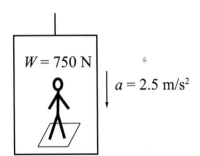

```
W = 750
a = 2.5
g = 10

# Formula: W = m*g

m = W/g

# Formula: Total_F = m*a --> W - Fn = m*a

Fn = W - m*a

print("The value on the scale is", Fn, "N")
```

The value on the scale is 562.5 N

25. A 2 kg mass is under three forces as shown in the figure below. What is the acceleration of the system?

$F_1 = 8\,N,\ F_2 = 6\,N,\ F_3 = 15\,N,\ m = 2\,kg$

Since the angle in between F_1 and F_2 is 90° their resultant can be found by pythagorean theorem.

$F_3 = 8$ N

$F_1 = 8$ N

37°

53°

$F_2 = 8$ N

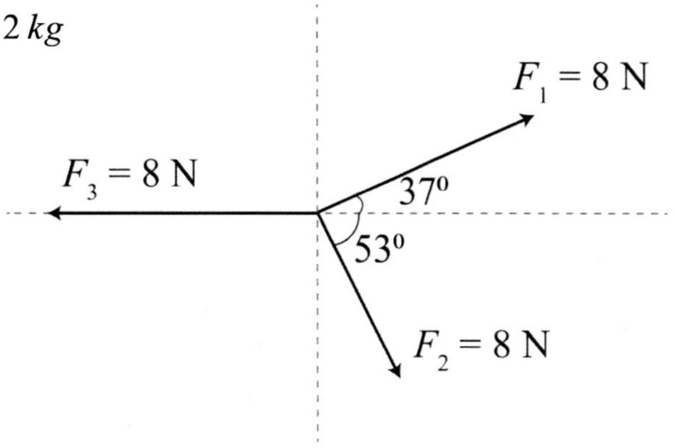

$$F_{1+2} = \sqrt{\left(F_1\right)^2 + \left(F_2\right)^2}$$

$$F_{1+2} = \sqrt{(8)^2 + (6)^2}$$

$$F_{1+2} = 10N$$

Resultant of F_1 and F_2 is parallel to F_3 and in the oposite direction so,

$$\Sigma F = ma$$

$$a = \frac{F_{1+2} - F_3}{m} = \frac{10 - 15}{2}$$

$$a = -2.5\ m/s^2$$

```python
import math

F1 = 8
F2 = 6
F3 = 15
m = 2
# Since the angle in between F1 and F2 is 90 degrees,
# their resultant can be found by pythagorean theorem

F1_2 = math.sqrt(F1**2 + F2**2)

# Resultant of F1 and F2 is parallel fo F3 and in the opposite direction,
# so Total_F = m*a

a = (F1_2 - F3)/m
print("The acceleration of the system is",a,"m/s^2")
```

The acceleration of the system is -2.5m/s^2

26. Force of 12 N and an unknown force are acting on 3 kg object in the same direction. If the acceleration of the object is 5 m/s², what is the magnitude of the unknown force?

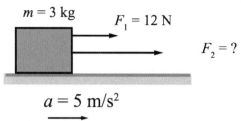

$F_1 = 12\,N,\ F_2 = ?$

$m = 3\,kg,\ a = ?$

$\Sigma F = ma,\ (F_2 + 12) = 3 \cdot 5$

$F_2 = 15 - 12,\ F_2 = 3\,N$

$a = 5$ m/s²

```
F1 = 12
m = 3
a = 5


# Formula: (F2 + F1) = m*a
F2 = m*a - F1
print("The magnitude of the uknown force is", F2, "N")
```

The magnitude of the uknown force is 3 N

27. An unknown mass is on a flat frictionless surface and a 2 kg object is attached to it with a string that is going over pulley which is mounted to the end of the table. Acceleration of the 2 kg object is 1.8 m/s . What is the mass of the object?

$m_2 = 2\,kg,\ a_{system} = 1.8\,m/s^2,\ m_1 = ?$

$\Sigma F = ma,\ m_2 g = (m_1 + m_2) \cdot a$

$m_1 = \dfrac{m_2 g}{a} - m_2,\ m_1 = \dfrac{2 \cdot 10}{1.8} - 2,$

$m_1 = 9.11\,kg$

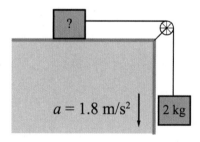

$a = 1.8$ m/s²   2 kg

```
m2 = 2
a = 1.8
g = 10

# Formula: Total_F = m*a --> m1*g = (m1 + m2)*a

m1 = (m2*g)/a - m2
print("The mass of the object is", round(m1,2), "kg")
```

The mass of the object is 9.11 kg

28. Two objects are pushed to the right with a force of 20 N on a smooth surface. What is the reaction force acting on 3 kg object?

$m_1 = 3\,kg, \quad m_2 = 2\,kg, \quad F_{system} = 20\,N$

$a_{system} = ?, \quad F_{2\,on\,1} = ?$

$\Sigma F_{sys} = m_{sys}\,a_{sys}$

$20 = (2+3) \cdot a_{sys}$

$a_{sys} = 4\,m/s^2$

$F_{1\,on\,2} = m_2 \cdot a_{sys}$

$F_{1\,on\,2} = 2 \cdot 4$

$F_{1\,on\,2} = F_{2\,on\,1} = 8\,N$

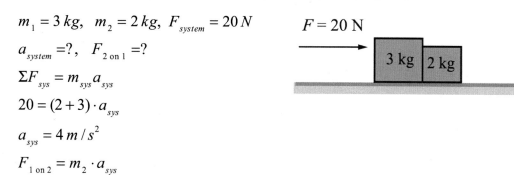

$F = 20\,N$

```
m1 = 3
m2 = 2
F_system = 20

# Formula: F_system = m_sys * a_sys

a_sys = F_system / (m1 + m2)

F1_2 = m2 * a_sys
print("The reaction force acting on 3 kg object is", F1_2, "N")
```

The reaction force acting on 3 kg object is 8.0 N

29. A 4 kg object is placed on a smooth inclined plane that is making 35^0 angles with the horizontal. What is the acceleration of the object, if there is no friction on the surface?

$\theta = 35°$, $m = 4\,kg$, $a = ?$

$F_g = mg$, $F_g = 40\,N$

$F_{g,x} = F_g \cdot \sin\theta$, $F_{g,x} = 40 \cdot \sin35$

$F_{g,x} = 22.94\,N$, $\Sigma F = ma$

$a = \dfrac{F_{g,x}}{m}$, $a = \dfrac{22.94}{4}$, $a = 5.73\,m/s^2$

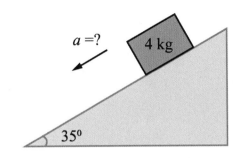

```
import math

angle = 35
m = 4
g = 10

Fg = m * g

Fg_x = Fg * math.sin(math.radians(angle))

# Formula: F = m*a

a = Fg_x/m

print("The acceleration of the object is",
      round(a,2),"m/s^2")
```

The acceleration of the object is 5.74 m/s^2

30. A cafe sign is balanced with two wires. One is parallel to the ground and the other is making 20° angle with the ceiling. Tension on the horizontal wire is 100 N. What is the mass of the sign?

$T_1 = 100\,N$, $\theta = 20°$, $T_2 = ?$, $m = ?$

$T_{2.x} = T_1$ $T_{2.x} = 100$, $T_{2.x} = T_2 \cdot \cos\theta$

$100 = T_2 \cdot \cos 20$,

$T_2 = \dfrac{100}{\cos 20}$, $T_2 = 106.42N$

$T_{2.y} = T_2 \cdot \sin\theta$, $T_{2.y} = 106.42 \cdot \sin 20$, $T_{2.y} = 36.40\,N$

$mg = T_{2.y}$,

$m = \dfrac{T_{2.y}}{g}$, $m = \dfrac{36.40}{10}$, $m = 3.64\,kg$

```
import math
T1 = 100
angle = 20
g = 10

T2x = T1

# Formula: T2x = T2 * cos(angle)

T2 = T2x / math.cos(math.radians(angle))

T2y = T2 * math.sin(math.radians(angle))

# Formula: m*g = T2y

m = T2y / g

print("The mass of the sign is", round(m,2),"kg")
```

The mass of the sign is 3.64 kg

31. A boy tied a 300 g stone to 1.5 m long rope and swinging it vertical. What is the minimum tangential velocity of stone when it is at the top if tension on the rope is zero?

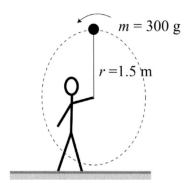

$m = 300$ g

$r = 1.5$ m

$$mg = ma_c$$
$$g = a_c$$

$$a_c = 10m/s^2$$

$$a_c = \frac{v_t^2}{r}$$
$$v_t = \sqrt{a_c \times r}$$
$$v_t = \sqrt{10 \times 1.5}$$
$$v_t = 3.87m/s$$

```python
import math

# Formula: m*g = m*a_c   -->  g = a_c

a_c = 10
r = 1.5

# Formula: a_c = v_t**2 / r

v_t = math.sqrt(a_c * r)
print("The minimum tangental velocity is",
      round(v_t,2),"m/s")
```

The minimum tangental velocity of stone is 3.87 m/s

32. If you walk around a circle of diameter 10 m, for 3π/2 rad, how far you have walked?

$$\Delta x = \theta \times r$$

$$\Delta x = \frac{3\pi}{2} \times 10m$$

$$\Delta x = 15\pi = 47.12m$$

```
import math
r = 10

angle = (3*math.pi)/2
dx = angle * r
print("Distance walked = ",round(dx,2),"m")
```

Distance walked = 47.12 m

33. A runner runs around a circular path with 10 m/s constant velocity. If he takes quarter of the path in 10 s, what is the angular velocity of the runner?

$$\omega = \frac{\Delta\theta}{\Delta t}$$

$$\omega = \frac{\frac{\pi}{4}}{10} = \frac{\pi}{40} = 0.078 rad/sec$$

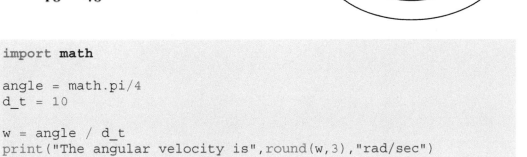

```
import math

angle = math.pi/4
d_t = 10

w = angle / d_t
print("The angular velocity is",round(w,3),"rad/sec")
```

The angular velocity is 0.079 rad/sec

34. A race car completes the first lap in circular road with radius 2000 m in 10 min. What is the angular and tangential velocity of a car?

$\omega = \dfrac{\Delta\theta}{\Delta t}$ (angular velocity),

$v = \dfrac{\Delta x}{\Delta t}$ (tangential velocity)

Then

$\omega = \dfrac{2\pi}{10 \cdot 60}$, $\omega = 0.0105 \, rad/s$

$v = \dfrac{2\pi r}{10 \cdot 60} = \dfrac{2\pi \cdot 2000}{10 \cdot 60}$, $v = 20.94 \, m/s$

```python
import math

# Formula (angular velocity): w = d_angle/dt
# Formula (tangential velocity): dx / dt

d_angle = 2*math.pi
r = 2000
dt = 10 * 60

w = d_angle/dt
v = d_angle * r / dt

print("The angular velocity is",round(w,4),
      "and the tangential velocity is", round(v,2))
```

The angular velocity is 0.0105 rad/s and the tangential velocity is 20.94 m/s

35. A fisherman is swinging fishing line 2 times before throwing it in 5 second. If the fishing line is 3 m, and mass of the hook is 100 g, what is the tension on the fishing line?

$$a_c = \frac{v_t^2}{r}, \quad a_c = \frac{\left(\dfrac{2 \times 2\pi r}{t}\right)^2}{r}, \quad a_c = \frac{\left(\dfrac{2 \times 2\pi 3}{5}\right)^2}{3} = 18.95 \, m/s^2$$

$$\text{Tension} + mg = m \times a_c$$
$$T + (0.1) \times 10 = (0.1) \times 18.95$$
$$T = 0.89 N$$

```python
import math

r = 3
angle = 2 * math.pi
t = 5
period = 2

# Formula: a_c = v_t**2 / r

v_t = period * angle * r /t
a_c = v_t**2 / r

# Formula: Tension + m*g = m * a_c
m = 0.1
g = 10

Tension = m * a_c - (m * g)

print("The tension on the fishing line is ",round(Tension,2),"N")
```

The tension on the fishing line is 0.89 N

36. A motorcycle, 1000 kg, comes to a hoop with 30 m/s velocity, then what is the normal force when the motorcycle is at the top?

We need to find tangential velocity at the top first.

$$E \cdot K_i + E \cdot P_i = E \cdot K_f + E \cdot P_f$$

$$\frac{1}{2}mv_i^2 + mgh_i = \frac{1}{2}mv_f^2 + mgh_f$$

$$v_f = \sqrt{v_i^2 - 2gh_f}$$

$$v_f = \sqrt{900 - 800} = \sqrt{100} = 10 \, m/s$$

$$F_N + mg = m\frac{v_f^2}{r}, \quad F_N = m\left(g - \frac{v_f^2}{r}\right)$$

$$F_N = 1000 \times \left(10 - \frac{100}{20}\right)N$$

$$F_N = 5000N$$

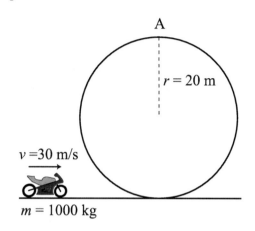

A

$r = 20$ m

$v = 30$ m/s

$m = 1000$ kg

```python
import math

# We need to find the tangential velocity at the top first

v_i = 30
g = 10
r = 20
h = 2*r
m = 1000

v_f = math.sqrt(v_i**2 - 2*g*h)

# Formula: F_N + m*g = m*(v_f**2)/r

F_N = m * (g - v_f**2/r)

print("The normal force is",round(F_N),"N")
```

The normal force when the motorcycle is at the top is 5000 N

37. A car, 1600 kg, is turning a curvature road which has a radius of 40m. If the coefficient of friction is 0.5, what is the maximum speed of the car that can turn the road without skidding off?

$$f_{friction} = m\frac{v_t^2}{r}, \; k \cdot F_N = m\frac{v_t^2}{r}$$

$$v_t = \sqrt{\frac{k \cdot F_N \cdot r}{m}}$$

where $F_N = mg$

$$v_t = \sqrt{k \cdot g \cdot r}$$

$$v_t = \sqrt{(0.5) \cdot 10 \cdot 40}$$

$$v_t = 14.14 m/s$$

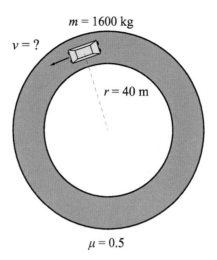

$m = 1600$ kg

$v = ?$

$r = 40$ m

$\mu = 0.5$

```python
import math

k = 0.5     #friction
g = 10
r = 40      #radius
m = 1600    #mass

# Formula:  f_friction = m * (v_t**2)/r
#           k * F_N = m * (v_t**2)/r
#           if F_N = m * g, so

v_t = math.sqrt(k*g*r)

print("The maximum speed of the car that can be",
      round(v_t,2),"m/s")
```

The maximum speed of the car that can be 14.14 m/s

38. A kid is rotating an object horizontal over his head with a speed of 4 m/s. If the length of rope is 1.2 m, and the object is 200 g, what is the tension on the string?

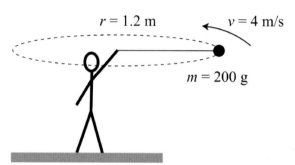

$r = 1.2$ m $\qquad v = 4$ m/s

$m = 200$ g

$m = 200\, g = 0.2\, kg$

$r = 1.2\, m,$

$v = 4\, m/s,$

$F = ?$

$$F = m\frac{v^2}{r}, \quad F = 0.2 \cdot \frac{(4)^2}{1.2}$$

$$F = 2.67\, N$$

```python
m = 0.2 # 200 gr = 0.2kg
r = 1.2
v = 4

F = m*v**2/r
print("The tension of the string is",round(F,2),"N")
```

The tension of the string is 2.67 N

39. The box is turning with 5 m/s velocity on a circular path. If the wall exerts 200 N force to 2 kg box, what is the radius of the rod? (No friction between box and rod)?

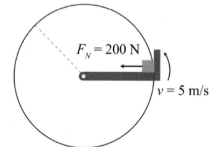

$F_N = 200$ N

$v = 5$ m/s

$$F_N = m\frac{v_t^2}{r}$$

$$200 = 2\frac{5^2}{r}$$

$$r = \frac{50}{200} = 0.25\, m$$

```python
v_t = 5
F_N = 200
m = 2

# Formula:  F_N = m * v_t**2 / r

r = m * v_t**2 / F_N
print("The radius of the rod is",r,"m")
```

The radius of the rod is 0.25 m

40. A 0.5 kg stone attached to a rope and is turning on a conical pendulum which has angle with axis. If the length of the rope is 2 m, what is the velocity of the stone?

$T_x = T \cdot \sin 30, \quad T_y = T \cdot \cos 30$

$T_y = mg, \quad T_x = m \dfrac{v_t^2}{r}$

$\dfrac{mg}{\cos 30} = \dfrac{m \dfrac{v_t^2}{r}}{\sin 30}$

$v = \sqrt{\dfrac{\sin 30 \cdot r \cdot g}{\cos 30}}$

$v = \sqrt{\tan 30 \cdot 1 \cdot \sin 30 \cdot g}$

$v = \sqrt{\tan 30 \cdot 10 \cdot 1}$

$v = 2.4 \, m/s$

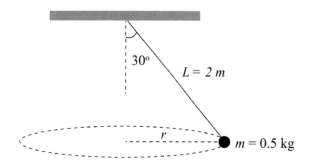

```python
import math

angle = 30
g = 10
m = 0.5
l = 2
r = l * math.sin(math.radians(angle))
# Fromula:
# T_x = T * sin(30) --> T_x = m * v_t**2 / r
# T_y = T * cos(30) --> T_y = m * g
# (m*g)/(cos(30)) = (m * v_t**2 / r)/(sin(30))

v_t = math.sqrt((math.sin(math.radians(angle))*r*g)
                /math.cos(math.radians(angle)))
print("The velocity of the stone is",round(v_t,2),"m/s")
```

The velocity of the stone is 2.4 m/s

41. A box is pushed by 50 N force as shown in the figure for 2 m. What is the work done by the force?

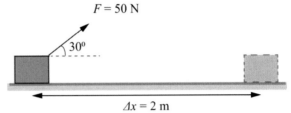

$F_x = F \cdot cos30$
$F_x = 50 \cdot cos30 = 43.30\ N$
$W = F_x \cdot d$
$W = 43.3 \cdot 2 = 86.6\ J$

```python
import math

F = 50
angle = 30
d = 2

F_x = F * math.cos(math.radians(angle))

W = F_x * d

print("The work done by force is",round(W,2),"J")
```

The work done by force is 86.6 J

42. A mass is raised 10 m in a given pulley system with 20 N force. What is the work done against gravity?

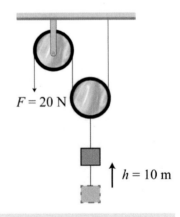

$2F = mg$
$mg = 2 \cdot 20 = 40\ N$
$W = mg \cdot d$
$W = 40N \cdot 10m = 400\ J$

```python
F = 20
d = 10

# Formula: 2F = mg

mg = 2 * F

# Formula: W = mg * d

W = mg * d

print("The work done against graviti is",W,"J")
```

The work done against graviti is 400 J

43. **2300 kg truck travels with 20 m/s constant velocity, what is the kinetic energy of the truck?**

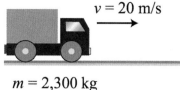

$v = 20$ m/s

$m = 2,300$ kg

$$KE = \frac{1}{2}mv^2$$

$$KE = \frac{1}{2} \cdot 2300 \cdot 20^2$$

$$KE = 460,000 \, J$$

```python
m = 2300
v = 20

# Formula: KE = (1/2) * m * v**2

KE = (1/2) * m * v**2

print("The kinetic energy of the track is",round(KE),"J")
```

The kinetic energy of the track is 460000 J

44. **10 kg bag is dropped from window of the building which is 25 m high. If we neglect the air resistance, what is the velocity of the bag when it hits the ground?**

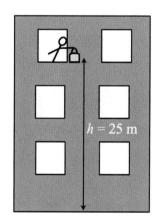

$h = 25$ m

$$PE_{initial} = KE_{final}$$

$$mgh = \frac{1}{2}mv^2$$

$$v = \sqrt{2gh}, \quad v = \sqrt{2 \cdot 10 \cdot 25},$$

$$v = 22.36 \, m/s$$

```python
import math
m = 10
h = 25
g = 10

# Formula: PE_initial = KE_final
# Formula: m*g*h = (1/2)*m*v**2

v = math.sqrt(2*g*h)
print("The velocity of th bag is",round(v,2),"m/s")
```

The velocity of th bag is 22.36 m/s

45. A 400 g ball is moving with 20 m/s constant velocity. A player hits the ball with 100 N force along with 30 cm. What is the final velocity of the ball?

$\Delta KE = W$

$$F \cdot d = \frac{1}{2}m(v_f^2 - v_i^2)$$

$$100 \cdot 0.3 = \frac{1}{2} \cdot 0.4 \cdot (v_f^2 - 20^2)$$

$$v_f^2 - 400 = \frac{30}{0.2}$$

$$v_f^2 = \sqrt{500} = 23.45\,m/s$$

$v = 20$ m/s

$m = 400$ g

```python
import math

m = 0.4
F = 100
d = 0.3
v_i = 20

# Formula: F*d = (1/2)*m*(v_f**2 = v_i**2)

v_f  = math.sqrt((2*F*d)/m + v_i**2)
print("The final velocity is",round(v_f,2),"m/s")
```

The final velocity is 23.45 m/s

46. The cart, 15 kg, is released from 15 m high platform, and stops at point C. If distance BC has friction, and AB is frictionless, what is the friction coefficient? (|BC|=30 m).

$\Delta E = W_{friction}$

$mgh = f_{friction} \cdot \Delta x$

$mgh = \mu \cdot mg \cdot \Delta x$

$\mu = \dfrac{h}{\Delta x}$

$\mu = \dfrac{15}{30} = 0.5$

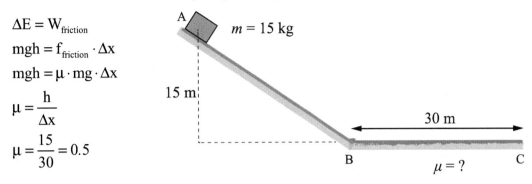

```
m = 15
dx = 30
h = 15


# Formula: dE = W_friction
# Formula: m*g*h = f_friction * dx
  where f_friction = friction_coef * m*g

friction_coef = h / dx
print("The friction coefficient is",friction_coef)
```

The friction coefficient is 0.5

47. A roller coaster starts its motion from point A with initial velocity 10 m/s. Assume that road is smooth, then what is the velocity of the train at point C?

$$KE_i + PE_i = KE_f + PE_f$$

$$\frac{1}{2}mv_i^2 + mgh_i = \frac{1}{2}mv_f^2 + mgh_2$$

$$\frac{1}{2}\cdot 10^2 + 10\cdot 20 = \frac{1}{2}\cdot v_f^2 + 10\cdot 10$$

$$50 + 200 = \frac{v_f^2}{2} + 100$$

$$v_f = \sqrt{300} = 17.32\,m/s$$

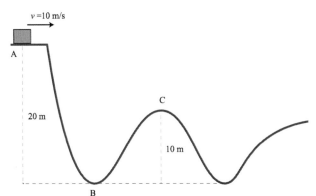

```
import math
import sympy as sym

h_1 = 20
h_2 = 10
g = 10
v_i = 10

# Formula: KE_i + PE_i = KE_f + PE_f
# Formula: (1/2)*m*v_i**2 + m*g*h_1 = (1/2)*m*v_f**2 + m*g*h_2
# if (m) is cancelled --> import sympy as sym (1/2)*v_i**2 + g*h_1 = (1/2)*v_f**2 + g*h_2

v_f = sym.symbols("v_f")

exp = (1/2)*v_i**2 + g*h_1 - (1/2)*v_f**2 - g*h_2

solution = sym.solve(exp)
print("The velocity of the train at the poin C is",
      round(solution[1],2),"m/s")
```

The velocity of the train at the poin C is 17.32 m/s

48. Jacob lifts 5 kg water by a crank from 9 m deep to ground level in 1 min. How much power does Jacob spend during that time?

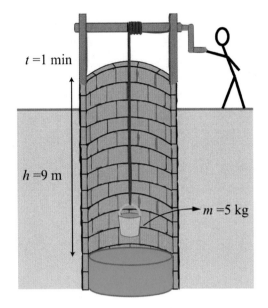

$m = 5\,kg$

$h = 9\,m$

$t = 1\,min = 60\,s$

$P = ?$

$P = \dfrac{W}{t} = \dfrac{mgh}{t}$

$P = \dfrac{5 \cdot 10 \cdot 9}{60}$

$P = 7.5\,Watts$

```
m = 5
h = 9
t = 60
g = 10

# Formula: P = W / t --> m*g*h / t

P = m*g*h / t
print("Jacob spends",P,"Watts power")
```

Jacob spends 7.5 Watts power

49. A car moves with 15 m/s constant velocity under effect of 1000 N force. How much power is generated by the engine of the car?

$P = \dfrac{F \cdot \Delta x}{\Delta t}$, where $v = \dfrac{\Delta x}{\Delta t}$. $P = F \cdot v$, $P = 1000 \cdot 15$, $P = 15000$ Watt

```
F = 1000
v = 15

# Formula: P = (F*dt) / dt, where v = dx/dt

P = F * v

print(P,"Watt is generated by the engine of the car")
```

15000 Watt is generated by the engine of the car

50. A clock generates 1W power to move pendulum from lowest point to the highest point. If the pendulum has mass of 100g and length of 50 cm, how long does pendulum take to reach maximum height?

$m = 100\,g = 0.1\,kg$

$P = 1\,Watt$

$L = 50\,cm = 0.5\,m$

$\theta = 30°$

$t = ?$

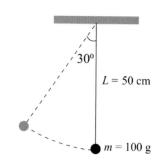

$$P = \frac{W}{t} = \frac{F \cdot \Delta h}{t} = \frac{mg \cdot \Delta h}{t}$$

$\Delta h = L - (L \cdot \cos \theta)$

$\Delta h = 0.5 - (0.5 \cdot \cos 30°)$

$\Delta h = 0.067\,m$

$$t = \frac{mg \cdot \Delta h}{P}$$

$$t = \frac{0.1 \cdot 10 \cdot 0.067}{1}$$

$t = 0.067\,s$

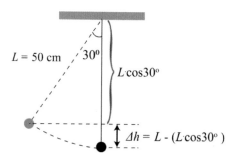

```
import math

m = 0.1
P = 1
L = 0.5
angle = 30
g = 10

# Formula: P = W /t ==> F*dh / t ==> m*g*dh/t

dh = L - (L * math.cos(math.radians(angle)))

t = m*g*dh / P

print("To reach maximum height, it will take",round(t,3),"s")
```

To reach maximum height, it will take 0.067 s

51. An electron has mass of kg, is moving with 6×10^6 m/s. What is the momentum of the electron?

$P_e = m_e \cdot v_e$

$P_e = 9.11 \times 10^{-31} \cdot 6 \times 10^6$

$P_e = 54.66 \times 10^{-25} \, kg \cdot m/s$

$v = 6 \times 10^6$ m/s

e⁻

$m = 9.11 \times 10^{-31}$ kg

```
v = 6 * 10**6
m = 9.11 * 10**(31)

P_e = m * v

print("The momentum of the electron is",P_e, "kgm/s")
```

The momentum of the electron is 5.466e+38 kgm/s

52. A 2 g bullet moves with 1250 m/s constant velocity. Then bullet hits the wooden block and sticks it. If the mass of block is 100g, then what is the final velocity of block and bullet together?

$P_{initial} = P_{final}$

$m_i \cdot v_i = m_f \cdot v_f$

$2 \times 10^{-3} \cdot 1250 = 0.102 \cdot v_f$

$v_f = \dfrac{2.5}{0.102} \quad P_e = 54.66 \times 10^{-25} \, kgm/s$

$v_f = 24.5 \, m/s$

$v = 1250$ m/s

$m = 2$ g

$m = 100$ g

$v = ?$

```
v_i = 1250
m_i = 2*10**(-3)
m_f = 0.102

# Formula: P_initial = P_final
# Formula: m_i * v_i = m_f * v_f

v_f = (m_i * v_i) / m_f

print("The velocity is",round(v_f,1),"m/s")
```

The velocity of the block and bullet together is 24.5 m/s

53. 200 g cart is released with no initial velocity from 1m height as shown in the figure below. When it hits the second cart, it stops. If the mass of second block is 400 g, what is the velocity of the second cart after collision? (Frictionless surface)

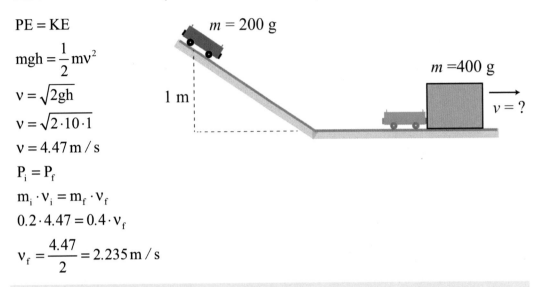

$$PE = KE$$

$$mgh = \frac{1}{2}mv^2$$

$$v = \sqrt{2gh}$$

$$v = \sqrt{2 \cdot 10 \cdot 1}$$

$$v = 4.47 \, m/s$$

$$P_i = P_f$$

$$m_i \cdot v_i = m_f \cdot v_f$$

$$0.2 \cdot 4.47 = 0.4 \cdot v_f$$

$$v_f = \frac{4.47}{2} = 2.235 \, m/s$$

```
m_i = 0.2
m_f = 0.4
g = 10
h = 1

# Formula: P*E = K*E
# Formula:  m * g * h = (1/2) * m * v_i**2

v_i = math.sqrt(2*g*h)

# Formula: P_i = P_f
# Formula: m_i * v_i = m_f * v_f

v_f = (m_i * v_i) / m_f

print("The velocity is",round(v_f,3),"m/s")
```

The velocity of the second cart after collision is 2.236 m/s

54. **Cart A, 200 g, moves due east with 6 m/s, and cart B, 300 g, moves due west with 8 m/s. After collision, cart A and cart B stick each other. What are the final velocity and direction of these two objects?**

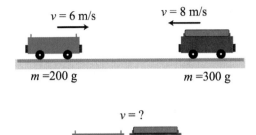

$m_A = 200\,g = 0.2\,kg$

$m_B = 300\,g = 0.3\,kg$

$v_{i,A} = 6\,m/s$

$v_{i,B} = -8\,m/s$

$v_f = ?$

$m_A \cdot v_{i,A} + m_B \cdot v_{i,B} = (m_A + m_B) \cdot v_f$

$$v_f = \frac{m_A \cdot v_{i,A} + m_B \cdot v_{i,B}}{(m_A + m_B)}$$

$$v_f = \frac{0.2 \cdot 6 + 0.3 \cdot (-8)}{(0.2 + 0.3)}$$

$v_f = -2.4\,m/s$

Negative sign represents west.

```
m_A = 0.2
m_B = 0.3
v_iA = 6
v_iB = -8

# Formula: m_A * v_iA + m_B * v_iB = (m_A + m_B) * v_f

v_f = (m_A * v_iA + m_B * v_iB) / (m_A + m_B)

print("The final velocity is",round(v_f,2),
      "m/s and direction of these two objects is West")
```

The final velocity is -2.4 m/s and direction of these two objects is West

55. A 50 kg person is standing on a frictionless ice with a 200 g ball in her hands. Then she throws the ball with a speed of 4 m/s forward. What is the velocity of the girl after she threw the ball?

$m_{girl} = 50\,kg$

$m_{ball} = 200\,g = 0.2\,kg$

$v_{i,girl} = 0\,m/s$

$v_{i,ball} = 0\,m/s$

$v_{f,ball} = 5\,m/s$

$v_{f,girl} = ?$

$m = 50\ kg$

$m = 200\ g$

$v = ?$ $v = 4\ m/s$

$m_{girl} \cdot v_{i,girl} + m_{ball} \cdot v_{i,ball} = m_{girl} \cdot v_{f,girl} + m_{ball} \cdot v_{f,ball}$

$50 \cdot 0 + 0.2 \cdot 0 = 50 \cdot v_{f,girl} + 0.2 \cdot 5$

$v_{f,girl} = \dfrac{-0.2 \cdot 5}{50}$

$v_{f,girl} = -0.02\,m/s$

```python
m_girl = 50
m_ball = 0.2
v_i_girl = 0
v_i_ball = 0
v_f_ball = 5

# Formula: m_girl * v_i_girl + m_ball * v_i_ball = m_girl * v_f_girl + m_ball * v_f_ball

v_f_girl = ((m_girl * v_i_girl + m_ball * v_i_ball)
           - (m_ball * v_f_ball)) / m_girl

print("The velocity of the girl is",v_f_girl, "m/s")
```

The velocity of the girl is -0.02 m/s

56. 1600 kg car moves with 18 m/s. The driver does not see the wall and hits and stops. What is the magnitude of the impulse during that collision?

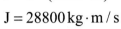
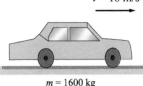

$v = 18$ m/s

$m = 1600$ kg

$J = \Delta P, \quad J = P_f - P_i$

$J = 0 - (1600 \cdot 18)$

$J = 28800 \, \text{kg} \cdot \text{m/s}$

```
m = 1600
v_i = 18
v_f = 0

# Formula: J = P_f - P_i --> (since the final velocity is zero, so P_f = 0)

J = m * v_f - m * v_i

print("The magnitude of the impulse is",
    J,"kgm/s")
```

The magnitude of the impulse during the collision is -28800 kgm/s

57. 58 gram tennis ball moves due east with 21 m/s. After the racket hits the tennis ball for 0.5 second, and tennis ball moves due west with 21 m/s. What is the force exerted by the racket?

$J = \Delta P, \quad F \cdot \Delta t = P_f - P_i$

$F \cdot (0.5) = m \cdot (v_f - v_i)$

$F \cdot (0.5) = (0.058) \cdot (21 - (-21))$

$F = 4.872 \, \text{N}$

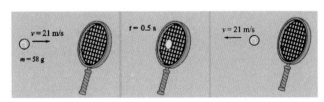

$v = 21$ m/s $\quad t = 0.5$ s $\quad v = 21$ m/s

$m = 58$ g

```
dt = 0.5
m = 0.058
v_i = -21
v_f = 21

# Formula: J = dP --> F * dt = P_f - P_i --> F * dt = m * (v_f - v_i)

F = m * (v_f - v_i) / dt

print("The forece exerted b the racket is",F,"N")
```

The forece exerted b the racket is 4.872 N

58. Mike Austin hits the 46 g golf ball with golf stick in 0.1 s. The ball flies 20 s and reaches 472 m world records. What is the force exerted by golf stick?

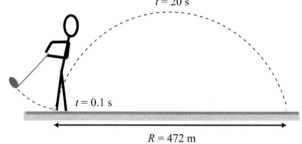

$$J = \Delta P, \ F \cdot \Delta t = m \cdot \Delta v$$

$$F \cdot \Delta t = m \cdot \frac{\Delta x}{\Delta t}$$

$$F \cdot (0.1) = (0.046) \cdot \frac{472}{20}$$

$$F = 10.856 \, N$$

```python
dt_i = 0.1
m = 0.046
dx = 472
dt_f = 20

# Formula: J = dP --> F * dt_i = m * dv --> F * dt_i = m *
dx/dt_f

F = (m * dx/dt_f) / dt_i

print("The force exerted by golf stick is",round(F,3), "N")
```

The force exerted by golf stick is 10.856 N

59. Force-time graph of a 5 kg object is given below. If object was at rest initially, what is the velocity of the object at the end of 5 s.?

$$A_1 = \frac{height \cdot base}{2} = \frac{20 \cdot 2}{2} = 20$$

$$A_2 = length \cdot height = 2 \cdot 20 = 40$$

$$A_{total} = A_1 + A_2 = 60$$

Area under F vs t graph represents change in momentum

$$\Delta p = 60 \, kg \cdot m/s$$

$$m \cdot (v_f - v_i) = 60$$

$$v_f = \frac{60}{m} + v_i$$

$$v_f = \frac{60}{5} + 0 = 12 \, m/s$$

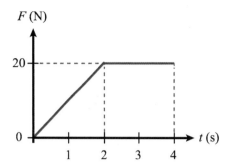

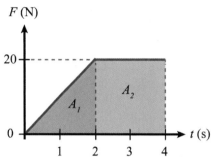

```
height = 20
length = 20
base = 2

Area_1 = height * base / 2
Area_2 = length * base
Area_total = Area_1 + Area_2

# The Area_total (graph under F vs t graph)
   represents change in momentum

dp = Area_total

v_i = 0
m = 5

# Formula: dp = m * (v_f - v_i)

v_f = dp/m + v_i

print("The velocity of the object is",round(v_f),"m/s")
```

The velocity of the object is 12 m/s

60. A 3 kg object that is moving with 4 m/s to the right collides head on with another identical object that is moving to the left with a velocity of 1.5 m/s. If they stick after the collision, what is the energy lost during the collision?

$$m_1 = 3\,kg, \quad m_2 = 3\,kg$$

$$v_{i,1} = 4\,m/s, \ v_{i,2} = -2\,m/s, \ \Delta E = ?$$

$$m_1 \cdot v_{i,1} + m_2 \cdot v_{i,2} = (m_1 + m_2) \cdot v_f$$

$$v_f = \frac{m_1 \cdot v_{i,1} + m_2 \cdot v_{i,2}}{(m_1 + m_2)}$$

$$v_f = \frac{3 \cdot 4 + 3 \cdot (-2)}{(3+3)}, \ v_f = 1\,m/s$$

$$\Delta E = E_f - E_i$$

$$\Delta E = \frac{1}{2} \cdot \left\{ \left[m_1 \cdot \left(v_{f,1} \right)^2 + m_2 \cdot \left(v_{f,2} \right)^2 \right] - \left[m_1 \cdot \left(v_{i,1} \right)^2 + m_2 \cdot \left(v_{i,2} \right)^2 \right] \right\}$$

$$\Delta E = \frac{1}{2} \cdot \left\{ \left[3 \cdot (1)^2 + 3 \cdot (1)^2 \right] - \left[3 \cdot (4)^2 + 3 \cdot (-2)^2 \right] \right\}$$

$$\Delta E = -27\,J$$

Negative represents the lost energy.

```
m_1 = 3
m_2 = 3
v_i1 = 4
v_i2 = -2

# Formula: m1 * v_i1 + m2 * v_i2 = (m1 + m2) * v_f

v_f = (m_1 * v_i1 + m_2 * v_i2) / (m_1 + m_2)

# Formula: dE = E_f - E_i

E_f = ((m_1*(v_f**2) + m_2*(v_f**2)))
E_i = ((m_1*(v_i1**2) + m_2*(v_i2**2)))

dE = (1/2)*(E_f - E_i)

if dE < 0:
    print("The energy lost is", dE,
          "J, Negative represents the lost energy")
```

The energy lost is -27.0 J, Negative represents the lost energy

61. **10 N force is applied to end of the massless level arm which is 1.5 m as shown in the figure. What is the total torque of the system?**

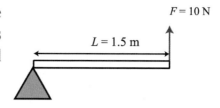

$T = F \cdot d$

$T = 10 \cdot 1.5 = 15 \, Nm$

```
F = 10
d = 1.5

T = F * d

print("The total torque of the system is", T, "Nm")
```

The total torque of the system is 15.0 Nm

62. **A worker is climbing the stairs to reach the roof of the house. If mass of the worker is 75 kg, what is the normal force on the the ground when worker is in the middle of the stairs?**

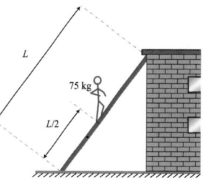

Due to transitional equilibrium, forces up must be equal to forces down.
So;

$F_{N,ground} = mg$

$F_{N,ground} = 75 \cdot 10 = 750 \, N$

```
m = 75
g = 10

F = m * g

print("The normal force is", F, "N")
```

The normal force is 750 N

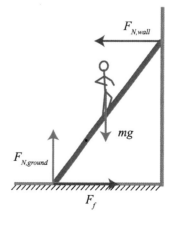

63. If the system is in balance, what is the mass of object X and Y?

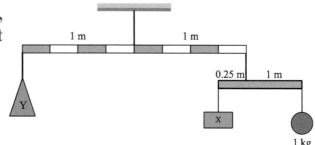

$m_x \cdot 0.25 = 1 \cdot 1$
$m_x = 4\ kg$
$m_y \cdot 1 = (m_x+1) \cdot 1$
$m_y = 4+1 = 5\ kg$

```
d1 = 0.25
d2 = 1
d3 = 1
d4 = 1

m2 = 1

mx = (d2*m2)/d1

# Formula: my * d4 = (mx + m2) * d3

my = ((mx + m2) * d3) / d4

print("The mass of object X is %s kg and the mass of
       object Y is %s kg" %(mx,my))
```

The mass of object X is 4.0 kg and the mass of object Y is 5.0 kg

64. If 100 N force is applied to 2 kg level arm as shown in the figure, what is the total torque of the system? (Length of the arm is 2 m)

$T_{total} = T_1 + T_2$

$T_{total} = (F \cdot sin53 \cdot 2) - (2 \cdot 10 \cdot 1)$

$T_{total} = 140\ N \cdot m$

```
import math

# Formula: T_total = T1 + T2

F = 100
d = 2
g = 10
m = 2
angle = 53

T_total = (F * math.sin(math.radians(angle)) * d) - (m * g )

print("The torque of the system is",round(T_total),"Nm")
```

The torque of the system is 140 Nm

65. A 50 kg block is pulled from the middle with force. To rotate the block from corner (labelled as X), what must be the minimum force?

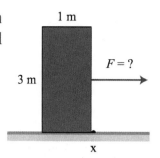

$F \cdot d_{force} = mg \cdot d_{center\,of\,mass}$

$F \cdot 1.5 = 50 \cdot 10 \cdot 0.5$

$F=166.7\ N$

```
d_force = 1.5
m = 50
g = 10
d_centerofmass = 0.5

# Formula: F * d_force = m*g*d_centerofmass

F = (m*g*d_centerofmass) / d_force

print("The minimum force must be",round(F,1),"N")
```

The minimum force must be 166.7 N

66. The signpost of the supermarket is suspended by two ropes as shown in the figure. If the signpost is 50 kg itself, what is the tension on the ropes?

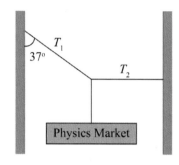

$$T_{1x} = T_2, \quad T_{1y} = mg$$

$$T_1 \cdot \sin 37 = T_2$$

$$T_{1y} = T_1 \cdot \cos 37 = mg$$

$$T_1 = \frac{mg}{\cos 37}$$

$$T_1 = \frac{50 \cdot 10}{\cos 37}$$

$$T_1 = 626 \, N$$

$$T_2 = T_{1x} = T_1 \times \sin 37$$

$$T_2 = 625 \cdot \sin 37$$

$$T_2 = 377 \, N$$

```python
import math

m = 50
g = 10
angle = 37

T_1y = m*g

# Formula: T_1y = T_1 * cos(37) = m*g

T_1 = (m*g) / math.cos(math.radians(angle))

T_2 = T_1 * math.sin(math.radians(angle))

print("The tension of ropes are %s N and %s N"
      %(round(T_1),round(T_2)))
```

The tension of ropes are 626 N and 377 N

67. **Two people are standing on the beam balance as in the figure. The first person is 50 kg and 2 m from middle of the balance. Second person is 75 kg and 0.5 m away from midpoint. What is the total torque of the system?**

50 kg   75 kg

2 m   0.5 m

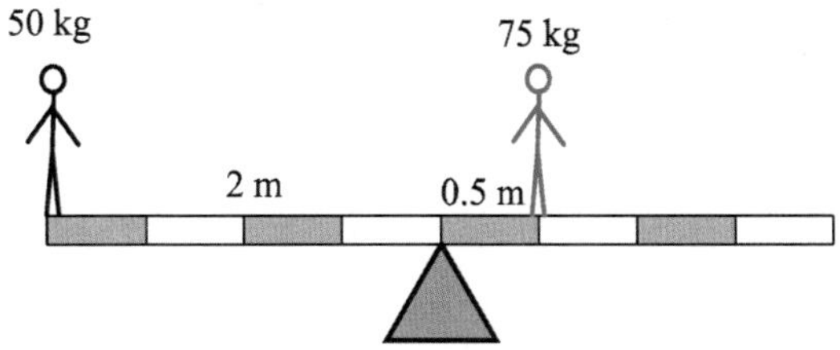

$T_{total} = T_1 + T_2$

$T_{total} = (50 \cdot 10 \cdot 2) - (75 \cdot 10 \cdot 0.5)$

$T_{total} = 625\ N \cdot m$

```
m1 = 50
d1 = 2
m2 = 75
d2 = 0.5
g = 10

T_1 = m1*g*d1
T_2 = m2*g*d2

T_total = T_1 - T_2
print("The total torque of the system is %s Nm"
      %(round(T_total)))
```

The total torque of the system is 625 Nm

68. A 200 g of mass is placed on the 20 cm mark and meter stick is hung at 30 cm mark. What is the mass of the meterstick if the system is balanced?

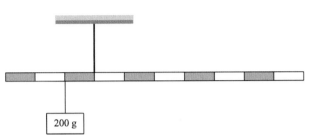

$m_1 = 200g$

$L = 1m$

$\ell = 20cm$

$CofM = 50cm$

$Pivot = 30cm$

$m_2 = ?$

$r_1 = pivot - \ell = 30 - 20$

$r_1 = 10cm$

$r_2 = CofM - pivot = 50 - 30$

$r_2 = 20cm$

$m_1 \cdot r_1 = m_2 \cdot r_2$

$m_2 = \dfrac{m_1 \cdot r_1}{r_2} = \dfrac{200 \cdot 10}{20}$

$m_2 = 100g$

```python
m1= 200
L = 1
l = 20

C_of_M = 50
Pivot = 30

r1 = Pivot - l

r2 = C_of_M - Pivot

# Formula: m1 * r1 = m2 * r2

m2 = (m1 * r1) / r2

print("The mass of the meterstick is %s g" %m2)
```

The mass of the meterstick is 100.0 g

69. A 60 kg person climbs up on a ladder that has a negligible mass. There is friction on the floor and not on the wall. Coefficient of friction on the floor is 0.4, length of the ladder is 4 m and the person is standing at 1m mark.

$m = 60kg, \ L = 4m$

$\ell = 1m, \quad \mu = 0.4$

$F_{N,1} = mg = 60 \cdot 10$

$F_{N,1} = 600N$

$F_f = F_{N,1} \cdot \mu = 600 \cdot 0.4$

$F_f = 240N$

$F_{N,2} = F_f, \ F_{N,2} = 240N$

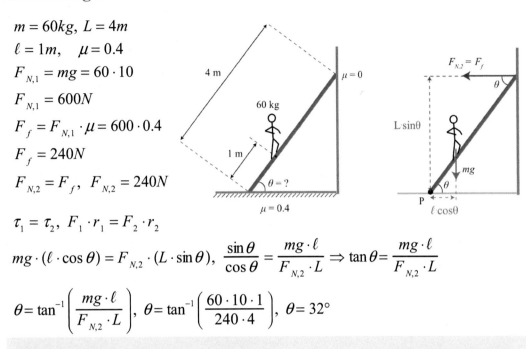

$\tau_1 = \tau_2, \ F_1 \cdot r_1 = F_2 \cdot r_2$

$mg \cdot (\ell \cdot \cos \theta) = F_{N,2} \cdot (L \cdot \sin \theta), \quad \dfrac{\sin \theta}{\cos \theta} = \dfrac{mg \cdot \ell}{F_{N,2} \cdot L} \Rightarrow \tan \theta = \dfrac{mg \cdot \ell}{F_{N,2} \cdot L}$

$\theta = \tan^{-1}\left(\dfrac{mg \cdot \ell}{F_{N,2} \cdot L} \right), \ \theta = \tan^{-1}\left(\dfrac{60 \cdot 10 \cdot 1}{240 \cdot 4} \right), \ \theta = 32°$

```
import math

m = 60
L = 4
l = 1
friction = 0.4
g = 10

F_N1 = m*g
F_f = F_N1 * friction
F_N2 = F_f

# Formula: F_1 * r_1 = F_2 * r_2
# Formula: m * g * (l * cos(angle)) = F_N2 * (L * sin(angle))
# Formula: sin(angle)/cos(angle) = (m*g*l)/(F_N2 * L) -->
tan(angle)=(m*g*l)/(F_N2 * L)

angle = math.degrees(math.atan((m*g*l)/(F_N2 * L)))

print("The angle is %s degrees"%round(angle))
```

The angle is 32 degrees

70. A 7 kg mass is suspended in the system as shown below. Radius of the big circle is 30 cm, and radius of the small circle is 10 cm. If system is in equilibrium, what is the magnitude value of the force?

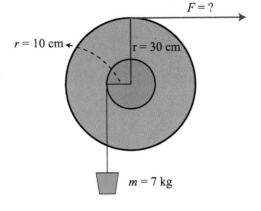

$F \cdot R = mg \cdot r$

$F \cdot 30 = 7 \cdot 10 \cdot 10$

$F = \dfrac{700}{30} N$

$F = 23.3 N$

```
R = 30
m = 7
g = 10
r = 10

# Formula: F * R = m*g*r

F = (m*g*r)/R
print("The magnitude value of the force is %s N" %round(F,1))
```

The magnitude value of the force is 23.3 N

71. What is the angular speed of a disc that is making 100 rev/min in rad/s?

$\omega = 100 \, rev/s \cdot \dfrac{2\pi \, rad}{1 \, rev} \cdot \dfrac{1 \, min}{60 \, s} = \dfrac{100 \cdot 2\pi \cdot 1}{60}$

$\omega = 10.47 \, rad/s$

$\omega = 100 \, rev/min$

```
import math

w = 100 * 2 * math.pi / 60
print("The angular speed of the disc is %s rad/s" %round(w,2))
```

The angular speed of the disc is 10.47 rad/s

72. A car is entering to a perfect circular loop with an angular speed of 20 rad/s. What is the Tangential speed of the car? Diameter of the circle is 30 m.

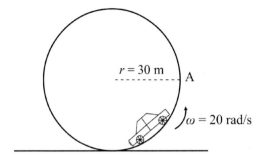

$\omega = 20\,rad/s$

$r = 30\,m$

$v_t = ?$

$v_t = \omega \cdot r$

$v_t = 20 \cdot 30$

$v_t = 600\,m/s$

```
w = 20
r = 30

v_t = w*r

print("The tangential speed of the car is %s m/s" %v_t)
```

The tangential speed of the car is 600 m/s

73. A wheel starts from rests to its rotation with an angular acceleration of 3 rad/s². What is the angular velocity of the wheel after 5 seconds?

$\alpha = 3$ rad/s² $t = 5$ s

$\omega_i = 0$ rad/s $\omega_f = ?$

$\omega_i = 0\,rad/s,\ \alpha = 3\,rad/s^2,\ t = 5\,s,\ \omega_f = ?$

$\omega_f = \omega_i + \alpha \cdot t,\ \omega_f = 0 + 3 \cdot 5,\ \omega_f = 15\,rad/s$

```
w_i = 0
alpha = 3
t = 5

w_f = w_i + alpha*t

print("The angular velocity of the wheel is %s rad/s" %w_f)
```

The angular velocity of the wheel is 15 rad/s

74. The diameter of a washing machine is 0.8 m. It accelerates with a tangential acceleration of 2 m/s² from rest. How long does it take for it to reach its peak angular speed of 23 rad/s?

$D = 0.8\,m,\ a = 2\,m/s^2,\ \omega_i = 0\,rad/s$

$\omega_i = 23\,rad/s,\ t = ?$

$r = D/2 = 0.8/2 = 0.4\,m$

$\alpha = \dfrac{a}{r},\ \ \alpha = \dfrac{2}{0.4} = 5\,rad/s^2$

$\omega_f = \omega_i + \alpha \cdot t$

$t = \dfrac{\omega_f - \omega_i}{\alpha},\ t = \dfrac{23 - 0}{5},\ t = 4.6\,s$

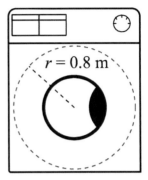

$r = 0.8\,m$

```
D = 0.8
a = 2
w_i = 0
w_f = 23

r = D/2
alpha = a/r

# Formula: w_f = w_i + alpha * t

t = (w_f - w_i)/alpha

print("To reach its peak angular speed, it takes %s seconds" %t)
```

To reach its peak angular speed, it takes 4.6 seconds

75. A sphere with a mass of 5 kg is attached to the end of a thread with no mass and rotated with a constant speed. What is the moment of inertia of the sphere if the length of the thread is 60 cm.

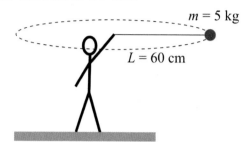

$m = 5kg$

$R = 60cm = 0.6m$

$I = mR^2$

$I = 5 \cdot (0.6)^2$

$I = 1.8 kg \cdot m^2$

```
R = 0.6

I = m*R**2

print("The moment of inertia is %s kg*m(square)"
      %round(I,1))
```

The moment of inertia os phe sphere is 1.8 kg*m(square)

76. A solid disk is rolling down on a table that is tilted 10°. What is the acceleration of the disc?

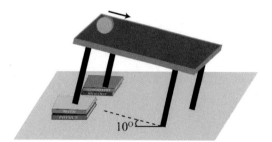

$\theta = 10°, \ a = ?$

$a = \dfrac{2}{3} g \sin \theta$

$a = \dfrac{2}{3} \cdot 10 \cdot \sin 10$

$a = 1.16 \, m/s^2$

```
import math

angle = 10
g = 10

alpha = (2/3) * g * math.sin(math.radians(angle))

print("The acceleration is %s m/s(square)"
      %round(alpha,2))
```

The acceleration of the disc is 1.16 m/s(square)

77. **A uniform wood stick with a length of 2 m and mass of 0.8 kg is able to rotate freely at one end that is mounted to a wall horizontally as shown. What is the angular acceleration of the stick if it is released from rest? I_{stick}=1/3ML^2**

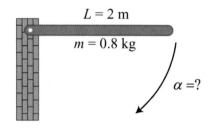

$$L = 2\,m,\ m = 0.8\,kg,\ \alpha = ?$$

$$I = \frac{1}{3}mL^2,\ I = \frac{1}{3} \cdot 0.8 \cdot (2)^2,\ I = 1.07\,kg \cdot m^2$$

$$\tau = mg \cdot \frac{L}{2},\ \tau = 0.8 \cdot 10 \cdot \frac{2}{2},\ \tau = 8\,N \cdot m$$

$$\alpha = \frac{\tau}{I},\ \alpha = \frac{8}{1.07},\ \alpha = 7.48\,rad/s^2$$

```
L = 2
m = 0.8
g = 10

I = (1/3) * m * L**2

torque = m*g*L/2

alpha = torque / I

print("The angular aceleration is %s rad/s(square)"
      %alpha)
```

The angular aceleration of the stick is 7.5 rad/s(square)

78. A string is rolled around a pulley with a diameter of 10 cm. Moment of inertia of the pulley is 0.04 kgm². The pulley is mounted to a table and. Then 2 kg of mass is attached at the end of the string and released off the table. What is the tension on the string?

$M = 0.3\,kg$

$D = 10cm = 0.1\,m$

$m = 2\,kg$

$I = 0.04\,kg \cdot m^2$

$T = ?$

$r = D/2 = 0.1/2 = 0.05\,m$

$T = \dfrac{mg}{1 + (mr^2/I)}$

$T = \dfrac{2 \cdot 10}{1 + (2 \cdot 0.05^2/0.04)}$

$T = 17.78\,N$

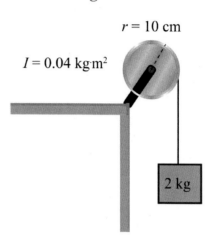

$r = 10\ cm$

$I = 0.04\ kg\cdot m^2$

2 kg

```
M = 0.3
D = 0.1
m = 2
I = 0.04
g = 10

r = D/2

T = (m*g)/(1+(m*r**2/I))

print("The tension of the string is %s N" %round(T,2))
```

The tension of the string is 17.78 N

79. London eye was opened to public in 2000 and it is Europe's tallest cantilevered observation wheel. Its core is like a hoop with a 135 m diameter and 1700 tons of mass. It accelerates with a constant rate and reaches to an angular speed of 1 rad/s in 15 seconds. What is the torque required to accelerate the system?

$$D = 135\,m, \ m = 1700000\,kg$$
$$\omega_i = 0\,rad/s, \ \omega_f = 1\,rad/s$$
$$t = 15\,s, \ \tau = ?$$
$$r = D/2 = 135/2 = 67.5\,m$$
$$I = \frac{1}{2}mr^2$$
$$I = \frac{1}{2} \cdot 1,700,000 \cdot (67.5)^2$$
$$I = 3,872,812,500\,kg \cdot m^2$$
$$\omega_f = \omega_i + \alpha \cdot t$$
$$\alpha = \frac{\omega_f - \omega_i}{t}, \ \alpha = \frac{1-0}{15}, \ \alpha = 0.067\,rad/s^2$$
$$\tau = I \cdot \alpha, \ \tau = 3,872,812,500 \cdot 0.067$$
$$\tau = 259,478,437.5\,N \cdot m$$

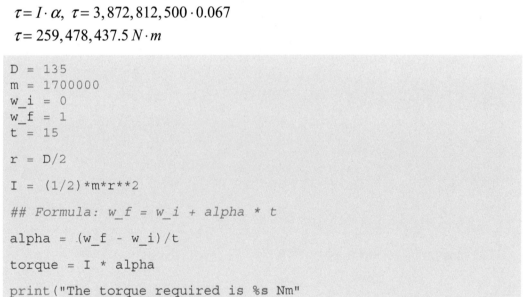

```
D = 135
m = 1700000
w_i = 0
w_f = 1
t = 15

r = D/2

I = (1/2)*m*r**2

## Formula: w_f = w_i + alpha * t

alpha = (w_f - w_i)/t

torque = I * alpha

print("The torque required is %s Nm"
      %round(torque))
```

258187500.0
The torque required to accelerate the system is 258187500 Nm

80. Rotational kinetic energy of a marble rolling with a constant speed is 120 J. If the radius of the marble is 0.1 m and the mass is 50 g what is the tangential speed of the marble? $I_{sphere} = 2/5MR^2$

$K = 120\,J,\ r = 0.1\,m,$

$m = 50\,g = 0.05\,kg,\ v_t = ?$

$I = \dfrac{2}{5}mr^2,\ I = \dfrac{2}{5} \cdot 0.05 \cdot (0.1)^2,$

$I = 0.0002\,kg \cdot m^2$

$K = \dfrac{1}{2}I\left(\dfrac{v_t}{r}\right)^2$

$v_t = r\sqrt{\dfrac{2K}{I}},\ v_t = 0.1\sqrt{\dfrac{2 \cdot 120}{0.0002}},$

$v_t = 109.54\,m/s$

$KE = 120\,J$

$r = 0.1\,m$

$m = 50\,g$

```python
import math

K = 120
r = 0.1
m = 0.05

I = (2/5) * m * r**2

# Formula: K = (1/2) * I * (v_t /r)**2

v_t = r * math.sqrt((2*K)/I)

print("The angular speed is %s m/s"
        %round(v_t,2))
```

The angular speed of the marble is 109.54 m/s

81. What is the angular momentum of soccer ball that is spinning with a speed of 20 rev/s. Estimate mass of a soccer ball is 454 g and its radius is 22 cm.

$$\omega = 20\,\frac{rev}{s} = 20\,\frac{rev}{s} \cdot \frac{2\pi\,rad}{1\,rev} = 125.66\,\frac{rad}{s}$$

$$m = 454\,g = 0.454\,kg$$

$$r = 22\,cm = 0.22\,m$$

$$L = ?$$

$$I = \frac{2}{5}mr^2,\ I = \frac{2}{5}0.454 \cdot (0.22)^2,\ I = \frac{2}{5}0.454 \cdot (0.22)^2$$

$$I = 0.00879\,kg \cdot m^2,\ L = I\omega,$$

$$L = 0.00879 \cdot 125.66,\ L = 1.10\,kg \cdot m^2/s$$

$\omega = 100$ rev/s

$r = 22$cm

$m = 454$ g

```python
import math

w = 20 * 2 * math.pi

m = 0.454
r = 0.22

I = (2/5) * m * r**2

L = I * w

print("The angular momentum is %s kg m^2/s"
      %round(L,2))
```

The angular momentum of soccer ball is 1.1 kg·m²/s

82. In a lab, students are trying to proof that angular momentum of an isolated system is conserved. They have a rotating platform which can spin with a constant angular speed and an object that can be moved away from the center on the rotating platform. They are also able to measure the speed of the object.
Their initial values are as follows.

Platform speed: 4 rad/s
Mass of the platform: 2 kg
Radius of the platform: 0.5 m.
Massobject : 1 kg
Rinitial: 0 m
RFinal: 0.25 m

What measurement of angular velocity can proof that angular momentum of an isolated system is conserved?

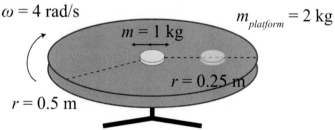

$$\omega_{i,P} = \omega_{i,O} = 4\frac{rad}{s}$$

$$m_P = 2\,kg,\; r_P = 0.5\,m,\; m_O = 1\,kg$$

$$r_{O,i} = 0\,m,\; r_{O,f} = 0.25\,m$$

$$I_P = \frac{1}{2}m_P R^2,\; I_P = \frac{1}{2}2\cdot(0.5)^2,\; I_P = 0.25\,kg\cdot m^2$$

$$I_{O,i} = m_O(r_i)^2,\; I_{O,i} = 1\cdot(0)^2,\; I_{O,i} = 0\,kg\cdot m^2$$

$$I_{O,f} = 1\cdot(0.25)^2,\; I_{O,f} = 0.0625\,kg\cdot m^2$$

$$I_{1,i}\omega_{1,i} + I_{2,i}\omega_{2,i} = \omega_f\left(I_{1,f} + I_{2,f}\right)$$

$$\omega_f = \frac{I_{1,i}\omega_{1,i} + I_{2,i}\omega_{2,i}}{\left(I_{1,f} + I_{2,f}\right)},\; \omega_f = \frac{0\cdot4 + 0.25\cdot4}{(0.0625 + 0.25)},\; \omega_f = 3.2\,rad/s$$

$$I_{1,i}\omega_{1,i} + I_{2,i}\omega_{2,i} = I_{1,f}\omega_{1,f} + I_{2,f}\omega_{2,f}$$

```
L_bar = 4
m_bar = 3
v_ball = 3
r_ball = 4
m_ball = 2
r_bar = 4

w_ball = v_ball / r_ball

I_ball = m_ball * r_ball**2

I_bar = (1/3)*m_bar*r_bar**2

I_bar_i = I_bar
I_ball_i = I_ball
I_bar_f = I_bar
I_ball_f = I_ball

w_bar_i = 0
w_ball_i = w_ball


# Formula: I_bar_i * w_bar_i + I_ball_i * w_ball_i = w_f *
(I_bar_f + I_ball_f)

w_f = (I_bar_i * w_bar_i + I_ball_i) /  (I_bar_f + I_ball_f)

print("The angular velocity is %s rad/s" %round(w_f,2))
```

The angular velocity is 0.67 rad/s

83. An object is attached to string and string passed through tube which allows to change the radius of the rotation. When the string can make a 1 m radius it is measured that objects speed is 5 m/s. What will be the speed if the string is pulled to 0.4 m of radius?

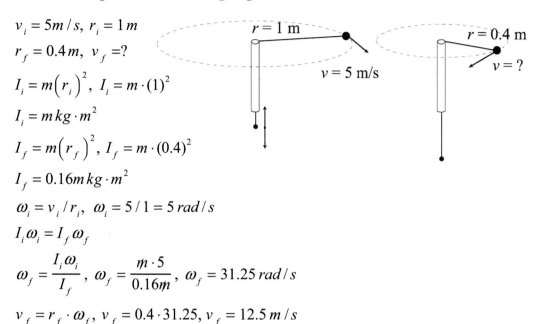

$v_i = 5 m/s,\ r_i = 1 m$

$r_f = 0.4 m,\ v_f = ?$

$I_i = m\left(r_i\right)^2,\ I_i = m \cdot (1)^2$

$I_i = m\,kg \cdot m^2$

$I_f = m\left(r_f\right)^2,\ I_f = m \cdot (0.4)^2$

$I_f = 0.16 m\,kg \cdot m^2$

$\omega_i = v_i / r_i,\ \omega_i = 5/1 = 5\,rad/s$

$I_i \omega_i = I_f \omega_f$

$\omega_f = \dfrac{I_i \omega_i}{I_f},\ \omega_f = \dfrac{m \cdot 5}{0.16 m},\ \omega_f = 31.25\,rad/s$

$v_f = r_f \cdot \omega_f,\ v_f = 0.4 \cdot 31.25,\ v_f = 12.5\,m/s$

```
v_i = 5
r_i = 1
r_f = 0.4
g = 10

# Formula: I_i = m * r_i**2 --> I_i = m * m**2
# Formula: I_f = m * r_f**2 --> I_f = 0.16m * m**2

I_i = 1
I_f = 0.16

w_i = v_i / r_i

# Formula: I_i * w_i = I_f * w_f --> w_f = (I_i * w_i)/I_f

w_f = (I_i * w_i)/I_f

v_f = r_f * w_f
print("The speed of the string will be %s m/s" %v_f)
```

The speed of the string will be 12.5 m/s

84. A bar with a length of 4 m and 3 kg of mass can rotate at one end of it freely as shown in the figure. A sticky ball is thrown towards the free end of the bar that is at rest. Velocity of the ball is 3 m/s and its mass is 2 kg. If the ball sticks to the bar what will be the angular velocity of the bar after the collision? $I_{bar} = 1/3 ML^2$

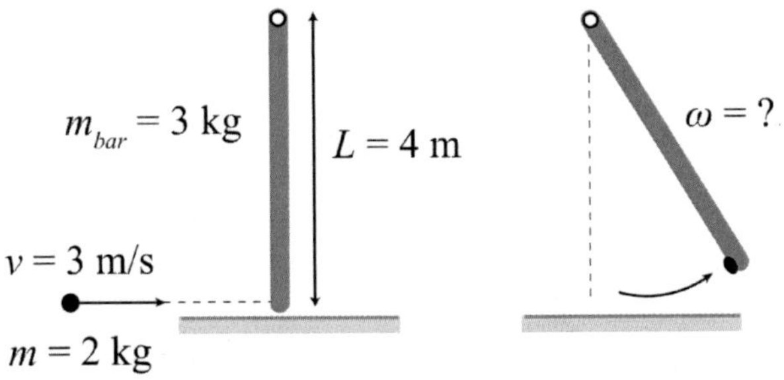

$$L_{Bar} = 4m, \ m_{Bar} = 3kg$$

$$v_{Ball} = 3m/s, \ r_{Ball} = 4m$$

$$m_{Ball} = 2kg, \ \omega_{Ball} = v_{Ball}/r_{Ball}$$

$$\omega_{Ball} = 3/4 = 0.75 \ rad/s$$

$$I_{Ball} = m_{Ball}\left(r_{Ball}\right)^2$$

$$I_{Ball} = 2\cdot(4)^2, \ I_{Ball} = 32 \ kg\cdot m^2$$

$$I_{Bar} = \frac{1}{3}m_{Bar}\left(r_{Bar}\right)^2, \ I_{Bar} = \frac{1}{3}\cdot 3\cdot(4)^2, \ I_{Bar} = 16 \ kg\cdot m^2$$

$$I_{Bar,i}\omega_{Bar,i} + I_{Ball,i}\omega_{Ball,i} = \omega_f\left(I_{Bar,f} + I_{Ball,f}\right)$$

$$\omega_f = \frac{I_{Bar,i}\omega_{Bar,i} + I_{Ball,i}\omega_{Ball,i}}{\left(I_{Bar,f} + I_{Ball,f}\right)}, \ \omega_f = \frac{16\cdot 0 + 32\cdot 0.75}{(16+32)}, \ \omega_f = 0.5 rad/s$$

$m_{bar} = 3$ kg $\quad L = 4$ m

$v = 3$ m/s

$m = 2$ kg

$\omega = ?$

```
L_bar = 4
m_bar = 3
v_ball = 3
r_ball = 4
m_ball = 2
w_bar_i = 0

w_ball_i = v_ball / r_ball

I_ball = m_ball * r_ball**2

I_bar = (1/3) * m_bar * r_ball**2

I_ball_i = I_ball
I_ball_f = I_ball
I_bar_i = I_bar
I_bar_f = I_bar

# Formula: I_bar_i * w_bar_i + I_ball_i * w_ball_i = w_f*(I_bar_f + I_ball_f)

w_f = (I_bar_i * w_bar_i + I_ball_i * w_ball_i)/(I_bar_f + I_ball_f)

print("The angular velocity of the bar is %s rad/s" %w_f)
```

The angular velocity of the bar is 0.5 rad/s

85. **A bar can rotate around its center freely. When it is rotating with an angular velocity of 4 rad/s. It hits a 3 kg of mass ball that is at rest on the table and the bar stops moving. What is the velocity of the ball after the collision? Length of the bar is 6 m and its mass is 2 kg. $I_{bar}=1/12ML^2$.**

$L_{Bar} = 6\,m,\ m_{Bar} = 2\,kg$

$r_{Ball} = L_{Bar}/2 = 6/2 = 3\,m,$

$m_{Ball} = 3\,kg,\ \omega_{Bar,i} = 4\,rad/s,$

$\omega_{Ball,i} = 0\,rad/s,\ \omega_{Bar,f} = 0\,rad/s$

$v_{Ball,f} = ?$

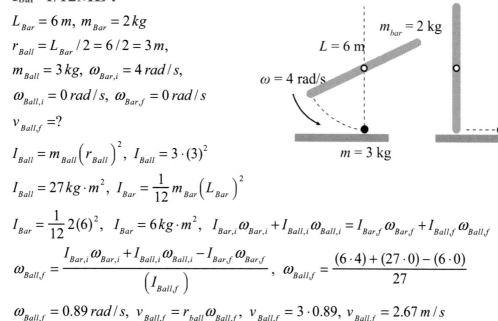

$I_{Ball} = m_{Ball}\left(r_{Ball}\right)^2,\ I_{Ball} = 3\cdot(3)^2$

$I_{Ball} = 27\,kg\cdot m^2,\ I_{Bar} = \dfrac{1}{12}m_{Bar}\left(L_{Bar}\right)^2$

$I_{Bar} = \dfrac{1}{12}2(6)^2,\ I_{Bar} = 6\,kg\cdot m^2,\ I_{Bar,i}\omega_{Bar,i} + I_{Ball,i}\omega_{Ball,i} = I_{Bar,f}\omega_{Bar,f} + I_{Ball,f}\omega_{Ball,f}$

$\omega_{Ball,f} = \dfrac{I_{Bar,i}\omega_{Bar,i} + I_{Ball,i}\omega_{Ball,i} - I_{Bar,f}\omega_{Bar,f}}{\left(I_{Ball,f}\right)},\ \omega_{Ball,f} = \dfrac{(6\cdot4)+(27\cdot0)-(6\cdot0)}{27}$

$\omega_{Ball,f} = 0.89\,rad/s,\ v_{Ball,f} = r_{ball}\omega_{Ball,f},\ v_{Ball,f} = 3\cdot0.89,\ v_{Ball,f} = 2.67\,m/s$

```
L_bar = 6
m_bar = 2

r_ball = L_bar/2
m_ball = 3
w_bar_i = 4
w_ball_i = 0
w_bar_f = 0

I_ball = m_ball * r_ball**2
I_bar = (1/12) * m_bar * L_bar**2

I_bar_i = I_bar
I_ball_i = I_ball
I_bar_f = I_bar
I_ball_f = I_ball

# Formula: I_bar_i * w_bar_i + I_ball_i * w_ball_i = I_bar_f * w_bar_f + I_ball_f * w_ball_f

w_ball_f = ((I_bar_i * w_bar_i) + (I_ball_i * w_ball_i) - (I_bar_f * w_bar_f))/I_ball_f

v_ball_f = r_ball * w_ball_f

print("The velocity of the ball is %s m/s"
%round(v_ball_f,2))
```

The velocity of the ball is 2.67 m/s

86. A thin stick that is 5 m long is suspended from its one end that is free to rotate and it is at rest. A toy car with a velocity of 4 m/s and mass of 2 kg hits to the other end of the stick and bounces back with 1 m/s of velocity. What is the angular momentum of the stick right after the hit?

$$\ell_{Stick} = 5\,m, \quad r_{car} = \ell_{Stick} = 5\,m, \quad m_{car} = 2\,kg,$$

$$L_{Stick,i} = 0\,kg \cdot m^2/s, \quad v_{car,i} = 4\,m/s$$

$$v_{car,f} = -1\,m/s, \quad L_{Stick,f} =?$$

$$\omega_{car,i} = \frac{v_{car,i}}{r_{car}}, \quad \omega_{car,i} = \frac{4}{5}$$

$$\omega_{car,i} = 0.8\,rad/s$$

$v = 4$ m/s

$m = 2$ kg

$L = 5$ m

$v = 1$ m/s

$\omega = ?$

$$\omega_{car,f} = \frac{v_{car,f}}{r_{car}}, \quad \omega_{car,f} = \frac{-1}{5}, \quad \omega_{car,f} = -0.2\,rad/s$$

$$I_{car} = m_{car}\left(r_{car}\right)^2, \quad I_{car} = 2 \cdot (5)^2, \quad I_{car} = 50\,kg \cdot m^2$$

$$I_{car,i}\,\omega_{car,i} + L_{Stick,i} = I_{car,f}\,\omega_{car,f} + L_{Stick,f}, \quad L_{Stick,f} = I_{car,i}\,\omega_{car,i} + L_{Stick,i} - I_{car,f}\,\omega_{car,f}$$

$$L_{Stick,f} = (25 \cdot 0.8) + 0 - \left[25 \cdot (-1)\right], \quad L_{Stick,f} = 45\,kg \cdot m^2/s$$

```python
l_stick = 5
r_car = 5
m_car = 2
L_stick_i = 0
v_car_i = 4
v_car_f = -1

w_car_i = v_car_i / r_car

w_car_f = v_car_f / r_car

I_car = m_car * r_car**2

I_car_i = I_car
I_car_f = I_car

# Formula: I_car_i * w_car_i + L_stick_i = I_car_f * w_car_f + L_stick_f

L_stick_f = (I_car_i * w_car_i + L_stick_i) - I_car_f * w_car_f

print("The angular momentum is", L_stick_f)
```

The angular momentum is 50.0

87. A platform is rotating with an angular speed of 5 rad/s. The mass of the platform is 3 kg and its diameter is 1 m. A clay of 400 g is dropped vertically straight down from top. The clay lands 0.3 m away from the center of the platform and sticks to the platform. What is the new angular velocity of the platform?

$$\omega_{i,P} = 5\frac{rad}{s}, \ m_P = 3\,kg$$

$$D_P = 1m, \ r_P = D_P/2 = 1/2 = 0.5\,m$$

$$m_{Clay} = 400g = 0.4\,kg, \ r_{Clay} = 0.3\,m$$

$$I_i = I_P = \frac{1}{2}m_P(r_P)^2$$

$$I_i = \frac{1}{2}3\cdot(0.5)^2, \quad I_i = 0.375\,kg\cdot m^2$$

$$I_{Clay} = m_{Clay}(r_{Clay})^2, \ I_{Clay} = 0.4(0.3)^2$$

$$I_{Clay} = 0.036\,kg\cdot m^2$$

$$I_f = I_P + I_{Clay}, \ I_f = 0.375 + 0.036, \ I_f = 0.411\,kg\cdot m^2$$

$$I_i\omega_i = I_f\omega_f$$

$$\omega_f = \frac{I_i\omega_i}{I_f}, \ \omega_f = \frac{0.375\cdot5}{0.411}, \ \omega_f = 4.56\,rad/s$$

$m = 400$ g

$\omega = 5$ rad/s

$r = 0.5$ m

$m_{platform} = 3$ kg

$r = 0.3$ m

$\omega = ?$

```
w_i_p  = 5
m_p = 3
D_p = 1

r_p = D_p/2
m_clay = 0.4
r_clay = 0.3

I_i = (1/2)*m_p*r_p**2
I_p = I_i

I_clay = m_clay * r_clay**2

I_f = I_i + I_clay

# Formula: I_i * w_i = I_f * w_f

w_f = I_i * w_i / I_f

print("The new angular velocity of the platform is %s rad/s"
      %round(w_f,2))
```

The new angular velocity of the platform is 4.56 rad/s

88. Moment of inertia of a disk is 10 kg/m^2 and it is rotating with and angular velocity of 100 rad/s. If it is dropped to another disk with a moment of inertia of 40 kg/m^2 that is it rest and stick to it, what will be the new angular velocity of the first disk?

$$\omega_i = \omega_{Disk1} = 100\frac{rad}{s}$$

$$I_{Disk1} = 10\,kg \cdot m^2$$

$$I_{Disk2} = 40\,kg \cdot m^2$$

$$I_i = I_{Disk1} = 10\,kg \cdot m^2$$

$$I_f = I_{Disk1} + I_{Disk2}$$

$$I_f = 10 + 40$$

$$I_f = 50\,kg \cdot m^2$$

$$I_i\omega_i = I_f\omega_f$$

$$\omega_f = \frac{I_i\omega_i}{I_f}$$

$$\omega_f = \frac{10 \cdot 100}{50}$$

$$\omega_f = 20\,rad/s$$

$I = 10$ kg/m^2

$\omega = 100$ rad/s

$\omega = 0$ rad/s $I = 40$ kg/m^2

$\omega = ?$

```python
w_i = 100
I_disk_1 = 10
I_disk_2 = 40

I_i = I_disk_1
I_f = I_disk_1 + I_disk_2

# Formula: I_i * w_i = I_f * w_f

w_f = I_i * w_i / I_f

print("The new angular velocity of the disk is %s rad/s"
      %round(w_f))
```

The new angular velocity of the disk is 20 rad/s

89. **A net torque is applied to a door for a 0.4 s and angular momentum of the door changes by 12 kg · m²/s. If the force is applied 0.5 m away from the hinges, what is the force applied?**

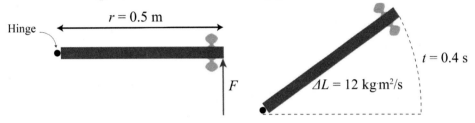

$t = 0.4\,s, \ \Delta L = 12\,kgm^2/s, \ r = 0.5\,m, \ F = ?$

$F = \dfrac{\Delta L}{r \cdot t}, \ F = \dfrac{12}{0.5 \cdot 0.4}, \ F = 60\,N$

```
t = 0.4
dL = 12
r = 0.5

F = dL / (r*t)

print("The force applied is %s N" %round(F))
```

The force applied is 60 N

90. **A metal sphere of mass 5 kg and radius 0.3 m rolls on a table without slipping. If the angular velocity of the sphere is 30 rad/s what is the linear momentum of the sphere?**

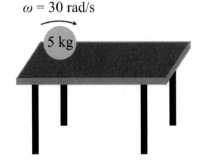

$\omega = 30\,rad/s$

$\omega = 30\,rad/s, \ m = 5\,kg$

$r = 0.3\,m, \qquad p = ?$

$p = mv, \ p = m(r\omega), \ p = 5 \cdot (0.3 \cdot 30),$

$p = 45\,kg \cdot m/s$

```
w = 30
m = 5
r = 0.3

# Formula: v = m*w
p = m * r * w

print("The linear momentum of the sphere is %s kg*m/s"
      %round(p))
```

The linear momentum of the sphere is 45 kg*m/s

91. What is the gravitational acceleration of a planet with a mass of 5.6×10^{27} kg and radius of 1.2×10^8 m?

$M = 5.6 \times 10^{27} \, kg, \ R = 1.2 \times 10^8 \, m$

$G = 6.67 \times 10^{-11} \, N \cdot m^2/kg^2, \ g = ?$

$g = \dfrac{GM}{R^2}, g = \dfrac{6.67 \times 10^{-11} \cdot 5.6 \times 10^{27}}{\left(1.2 \times 10^8\right)^2}, g = 25.94 \, m/s^2$

```
M = 5.6 * 10**27
G = 6.67 * 10**(-11)
R = 1.2 * 10**8

g = (G*M)/(R**2)

print("The gravitatonal acceleration is %s m/s(square)"
    %round(g,2))
```

The gravitatonal acceleration of the planet is 25.94 m/s(square)

92. A 5 kg object is dropped from certain height on earth. What is the acceleration of the earth toward the object?

$m = 5 \, kg, \ M = 6 \times 10^{24} \, kg$

$g = 10 \, m/s^2, \ mg = Ma$

$a = \dfrac{mg}{M}, a = \dfrac{5 \cdot 10}{6 \times 10^{24}}, a = 8.3 \times 10^{-24} \, m/s^2$

```
m - 5
M = 6 * 10**24
g = 10

# Formula: m * g = M * a
a = m*g/M

print("The acceleration of the Earth is %s m/s(square)" %a)
```

The acceleration of the Earth is 8.333333333333333e-24 m/s(square)

93. **The sun has a mass of 2.0×10^{30} kg and a radius of 7.0×10^5 km. What is the force on a 1000 kg object at the surface of the Sun?**

$$M = 2 \times 10^{30} \, kg, \; R = 7 \times 10^8 \, m$$

$$m = 1000 kg, \; G = 6.67 \times 10^{-11} \, \text{N} \cdot \text{m}^2/\text{kg}^2$$

$$F = G \frac{M \cdot m}{R^2}, \; F = 6.67 \times 10^{-11} \frac{2 \times 10^{30} \cdot 1000}{\left(7 \times 10^8\right)^2}, \; F = 2.7 \times 10^5 N$$

```
M = 2 * 10**30
R = 7 * 10**8
m = 1000
G = 6.67 * 10**(-11)

F = G*((M*m)/(R**2))

print("The force on a 1000 kg is %s N" %F)
```

The force on a 1000 kg object at the surface of the Sun is 272244.89795918367N

94. **The moon has a mass of 7.35×10^{22} kg and a radius of 1.74×10^6 m. What is the weight of an 85 kg astronaut on the moon?**

$$M = 7.35 \times 10^{22} \, kg, \; R = 1.74 \times 10^6 \, m, \; m = 85 \, kg$$

$$G = 6.67 \times 10^{-11} \, \text{N} \cdot \text{m}^2/\text{kg}^2, \; W = ?$$

$$g = \frac{GM}{R^2}, \; g = \frac{6.67 \times 10^{-11} \cdot 7.35 \times 10^{22}}{\left(1.74 \times 10^6\right)^2}, \; g = 1.62 \, m/s^2$$

$$W = mg, \; W = 85 \cdot 1.62, \; W = 138 \, N$$

```
M = 7.35 * 10**22
R = 1.74 * 10**6
m = 85
G = 6.67 * 10**(-11)

g = G*M/R**2

W = m*g

print("The weight is %s N" %round(W))
```

The weight is 138 N

95. Suppose the gravitational force between two massive spheres is 100 N. If the distance between the spheres is doubled, what is the force between the masses?

$$F = 100N,\ R = x,\ R_{new} = 2x$$

$$F_{new} = \frac{F}{\left(R_{new}/R\right)^2},\ F_{new} = \frac{100}{(2x/x)^2},\ F_{new} = 25N$$

```
F = 100
R = 1
R_new = 2 * R

F_new = F/ (R_new/R)**2

print("The force between two masses is %s N" %round(F_new))
```

The force between two masses is 25 N

96. A satellite is in a circular orbit around a planet that has mass of 4.6×10^{23}kg. Distance between the satellite and the center of the planet is 6×10^7 m. What should be the velocity of the satellite so that it can stay in the orbit?

$v = ?$

$$M = 4.5 \times 10^{23}\ kg,\ R = 6 \times 10^7\ m$$

$$G = 6.67 \times 10^{-11}\ N \cdot m^2/kg^2,\ v = ?$$

$$v = \sqrt{\frac{GM}{R}},\ v = \sqrt{\frac{6.67 \times 10^{-11} \cdot 4.5 \times 10^{23}}{6 \times 10^7}}$$

$$v = 707.28\ m/s$$

$d = 6 \times 10^6$ m

$m = 4.6 \times 10^{23}$ kg

```
import math

M = 4.5 * 10**23
R = 6 * 10**7
G = 6.67 * 10**(-11)

v = math.sqrt(G*M/R)

print("The velocity of the satellite should be %s m/s" %round(v,2))
```

The velocity of the satellite should be 707.28 m/s

97. What is the force in between the Sun and the Saturn?
m_{Sun}: 2.0×10^{30} kg, m_{Saturn} : 5.67×10^{26} kg, $D_{Sun \ and \ Saturn}$: 1.5×10^{12} m

$$M_{Sun} = 2 \times 10^{30} \ kg, \ M_{Saturn} = 5.67 \times 10^{26} \ kg$$

$$R = 1.5 \times 10^{12} \ m, \ G = 6.67 \times 10^{-11} \ N \cdot m^2/kg^2$$

$$F = G \frac{M_{Sun} \cdot M_{Saturn}}{R^2}, \ F = 6.67 \times 10^{-11} \frac{2 \times 10^{30} \cdot 5.67 \times 10^{26}}{\left(1.5 \times 10^{12}\right)^2}, \ F = 3.36 \times 10^{22} N$$

```
M_sun = 2 * 10**30
M_saturn = 5.67 * 10**26
R = 1.5 * 10**12
G = 6.67 * 10**(-11)

F = G * (M_sun * M_saturn)/R**2

print("The force in between the Sun and the Saturn is %s N" %F)
```

The force in between the Sun and the Saturn is 3.36168e+22 N

98. What is the minimum speed needed to escape from earths gravitational field? Assume mass of the earth is 6×10^{24} kg and radius is 6.37×10^6 m.

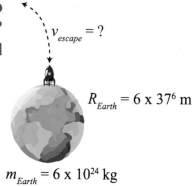

$$M = 6 \times 10^{24} \ kg, \ R = 6.37 \times 10^6 \ m,$$

$$G = 6.67 \times 10^{-11} \ N \cdot m^2/kg^2, \ v_{escape} = ?$$

$$v_{escape} = \sqrt{\frac{2GM}{R}}$$

$$v_{escape} = \sqrt{\frac{2 \cdot 6.67 \times 10^{-11} \cdot 6 \times 10^{24}}{6.37 \times 10^6}}, \ v_{escape} = 11,209.44 \ m/s$$

```
import math

M = 6 * 10**24
R = 6.37 * 10**6
G = 6.67 * 10**(-11)

v_escape = math.sqrt(2*G*M/R)

print("The minimum speeed needed is %s m/s" %v_escape)
```

The minimum speeed needed is 11209.43760256406 m/s

99. **A new planet is discovered and it mass is half of earth's mass the radius is one third of earths radius. What would an object that weights 500 N on earth weigh on this new planet? Gravitational acceleration on earth is 10 m/s^2.**

$$W_{earth} = 500\,N$$

$$R_{earth} = x,\ R_{new} = x/3,$$

$$M_{earth} = y,\ M_{new} = y/2,$$

$$g_{earth} = 10\,m/s^2,$$

$$W_{new} = ?$$

$$g_{new} = g_{earth}\,\frac{M_{new}/M_{earth}}{\left(R_{new}/R_{earth}\right)^2}$$

$$g_{new} = 10\,\frac{\frac{y}{2}/y}{\left(\frac{x}{3}/x\right)^2},\ g_{new} = 45\,m/s^2$$

$$m = \frac{W_{earth}}{g_{earth}} = \frac{500}{10},\ m = 50\,kg$$

$$W_{new} = mg_{new},\ W_{new} = 50\cdot 45,\ W_{new} = 2250\,N$$

```
W_earth = 500
R_earth = 1
R_new = R_earth / 3
M_earth = 1
M_new = M_earth / 2
g_earth = 10

g_new = g_earth * (M_new/M_earth)/(R_new/R_earth)**2

m = W_earth / g_earth

W_new = m*g_new
print("The weight would be %s N" %W_new)
```

The weight would be 2250.0 N

100. Weight of an apple on Jupiter is 600 N. Gravitational accelerations on Jupiter is calculated as 25 N/kg. What is the mass of this object on earth?

$$W_{Jupiter} = 600\,N$$

$$g_{Jupiter} = 25\,m/s^2$$

$$m = ?$$

$$m = \frac{W_{Jupiter}}{g_{Jupiter}} = \frac{600}{25}$$

$$m = 24\,kg$$

```python
W_jupiter = 600
g_jupiter = 25

m = W_jupiter / g_jupiter

print("The mass of object is %s kg" %round(m))
```

The mass of object is 24 kg

About the Authors

Tayyip Oral

Tayyip Oral is a mathematician and test prep expert who has been teaching in learning centers and high school test since 1998. Mr. Oral is the founder of 555 math book series which includes variety of mathematics books. Tayyip Oral graduated from Qafqaz university with a Bachelor`s degree in Industrial Engineering. He later received his Master`s degree in Business Administration from the same university. He is an educator who has written several SAT Math, ACT Math, Geometry, Math counts and Math IQ books. He lives in Houston,TX.

Farukh Khalilov

Farukh Khalilov received a Bachelor's Degree in Engineering and Master's Degree in Computer Science (USA). He has been working with middle and high school students for over a decade as a Math and Computer Science teacher in different continents (USA, Europe and Africa). He is a big fan of Data Science and Machine Learning as well as willing to implement Python programming language in a variety of subjects.

Bilal Sengez

Bilal Sengez has been teaching all levels of high school physics including AP Physics C, calculus-based college level physics, for eight years. He received his bachelor's degree in Physics. He is currently physics curriculum director in his school system. Mr. Sengez has been given summer teacher trainings in his school district for the past six years. He is also a rocket club mentor.

Fatih Narin

Fatih Narin graduated from Middle East Technical University with a Master of Science degree in Physics Education department. He has worked in South Korea, China, HongKong SAR, Uganda, and Canada as a mathematics and physics teacher.

Books by Tayyip Oral

1. Sheryl Knight, Mesut Kizil, Tayyip Oral, TSI MATH Texas Success Initiative, (1092 Questions with Answers), 2017

2. Tayyip Oral, Osman Kucuk, Hasan Tursu, Geometry for SAT & ACT (555 Questions with Answers), 2017

3. Tayyip Oral, Ferhad Kirac, Bekir Inalhan, Algebra for The New SAT, Level – 1, (1111 Questions with Answers), 2017

4. Kristin Alexander, Tayyip Oral, Sait Yanmis, 555 Gifted and Talented, Question Sets for the Mathematically Gifted Middle Grade Scholar (1111 Questions with Answers), 2017

5. Steve Warner, Tayyip Oral, Sait Yanmis, 1000 Logic&Reasoning Questions for Gifted and Talented Elementary School Students, 2017

6. Tayyip Oral, 555 ACT Math, 1110 Questions with Solutions, 2017

7. Tayyip Oral, 555 Math IQ for Elementary School Students (1270 Questions with Answers), Second Edition, 2017

8. Tayyip Oral, Ersin Demirci, 555 SAT Math, 2016

9. Tayyip Oral, 555 Geometry (555 Questions with Solutions), 2016

10. Tayyip Oral, Dr. Steve Warner. 555 Math IQ Questions for Middle School Students: Improve Your Critical Thinking with 555 Questions and Answer, 2015

11. Tayyip Oral, Dr. Steve Warner, Serife Oral, Algebra Handbook for Gifted Middle School Students, 2015

12. Tayyip Oral, Geometry Formula Handbook, 2015

13. Tayyip Oral, Dr. Steve Warner, Serife Oral, 555 Geometry Problems for High School Students: 135 Questions with Solutions, 2015

14. Tayyip Oral, Sevket Oral, 555 Math IQ questions for Elementary School Student, 2015

15. Tayyip Oral, Dr. Steve Warner, 555 Advanced math problems, 2015

16. Tayyip Oral, IQ Intelligence Questions for Middle and High School Students, 2014

21. T. Oral, E. Seyidzade, Araz publishing, Master's Degree Program Preparation (IQ), Cag Ogretim, Araz Courses, Baku, Azerbaijan, 2010.
    A master's degree program preparation text book for undergraduate students in Azerbaijan.

22. T. Oral, M. Aranli, F. Sadigov and N. Resullu, Resullu Publishing, Baku, Azerbaijan - 2012 (3rd. edition)
    A text book for job placement exam in Azerbaijan for undergraduate and post undergraduate students in Azerbaijan.

23. T. Oral and I. Hesenov, Algebra (Text book), Nurlar Printing and Publishing, Baku, Azerbaijan, 2001.
A text book covering algebra concepts and questions with detailed explanations at high school level in Azerbaijan.

24. T.Oral, I.Hesenov, S.Maharramov, and J.Mikaylov, Geometry (Text book), Nurlar Printing and Publishing, Baku, Azerbaijan, 2002.
A text book for high school students to prepare them for undergraduate education in Azerbaijan.

25. T. Oral, I. Hesenov, and S. Maharramov, Geometry Formulas (Text Book), Araz courses, Baku, Azerbaijan, 2003.
A text book for high school students' university exam preparation in Azerbaijan.

26. T. Oral, I. Hesenov, and S. Maharramov, Algebra Formulas (Text Book), Araz courses, Baku, Azerbaijan, 2000
A university exam preparation text book for high school students in Azerbaijan.

Made in the USA
Columbia, SC
07 April 2022

58626804R00095